Homework and Kids:
A Parent's Guide

School Support Series

By William Haggart
and Christine Juhasz

Performance Learning Systems
Nevada City, California

Performance Learning Systems, Publications Division, Arlington, TX 76013
© 2002 by Performance Learning Systems, Inc.
All rights reserved. Published 2002
Printed in the United States of America
10 9 8 7 6 5 4 3 2 1

Unless specifically stated as real in the text, similarity to real names and/or events is purely coincidental.

PLS Bookstore
224 Church Street
Nevada City, CA 95959
www.plsbookstore.com
info@plsbookstore.com
800-506-9996

Library of Congress Cataloging-in-Publication Data

Haggart, William, 1951-
  Homework and kids : a parent's guide / by William Haggart and Christine Juhasz.
    p. cm. — (School support series)
  Includes bibliographical references.
  ISBN 1-892334-12-7 (pbk. : alk. paper)
  1. Homework. 2. Education—Parent participation. 3. Cognitive styles in children. I. Juhasz, Christine, 1971- II. Title. III. Series.
  LB1048 .H35 2002
  372.13'028'1—dc21
                                    2002000179

ISBN 1-892334-12-7

Cover design, interior design, and illustrations: The Design Group

This book may be ordered from the PLS Bookstore, 224 Church Street, Nevada City, CA 95959, 800-506-9996. Quantity discounts are available for bulk purchases, sales promotions, premiums, fund-raising, and educational needs.

Contents

Part I:

Chapter 1

Chapter 2

Chapter 3

Chapter 4

Chapter 5

Part II:

Chapter 6

Chapter 7

Chapter 8

Chapter 9

Conclusion

References

The Kaleidoscope Profile®

Note: About The Kaleidoscope Profile®

To get the greatest benefits from this book, it is recommended that you and your child take The Kaleidoscope Profile®. The Kaleidoscope Profile® is a tool revealing your "learning styles" or the way you and your child learn best when you are learning something new. You will discover your and your child's learning styles as well as your respective approaches to school or work. You will also learn how your child approaches homework assignments.

You and your child should know your learning styles by the time you reach Chapter 3. There are two ways you can take The Kaleidoscope Profile®. You can order a paper version from Performance Learning Systems by calling 1-800-506-9996 (Pacific Time, Monday through Friday) or by visiting www.plsbookstore.com, or you can access The Kaleidoscope Profile® free online at www.plsweb.com.

The results of The Kaleidoscope Profile® will tell you about your learning styles or sensory preferences (the senses you use when you learn something new). This book focuses on the four sensory preferences or learning styles listed below:

- Visual: learns best by seeing, watching, reading.

- Auditory: learns by hearing, speaking, discussing, thinking aloud.

- Kinesthetic: learns while moving, doing things.

- Tactual: learns best by touch and feel, by relationship, emotion.

Once you know your own and your child's learning styles, you can make homework assignments easier and more enjoyable by taking into account your child's learning needs.

Once your child takes The Kaleidoscope Profile®, you will:

- Understand how your child learns and communicates.

- Recognize what your child values about learning and school.

- Develop worthwhile strategies for helping your child with homework.

- Discover how your individual learning style differs from your child's.

- Increase your child's desire to learn and enhance his or her self-confidence in performing schoolwork.

This book has assignments and activities to stimulate all four learning styles. Most people have a dominant learning style. After your child takes The Kaleidoscope Profile®, you may find that he or she has a nearly equal balance of two learning styles. The activities can easily be altered to address his or her specific needs.

By using the activities and suggestions that follow, your child will get the most from homework assignments. Experiment and have fun as you learn about your child and yourself.

INTRODUCTION

"Parents have a greater effect on their children's success in school than teachers or actual school programs."

— William Haggart, Educator and Author

Children are powerful learners. Without any prior experience or formal training, they learn how to apply concepts and use sounds to speak and communicate with others. This is a major accomplishment in learning!

In other words, children know how to learn.

Children do not need to be taught how to learn. By the time most children enter school, they already have an impressive "learning track record." With the right support from you during your child's school years, he or she can beat this record.

To succeed in school, children need **support**. They need **encouragement** to become responsible and independent learners. Most importantly, they need **confidence** that such support will enhance their own efforts to learn. These aids help children become lifelong learners. This book can be a vital tool in supporting your child as a learner.

You may find that you can apply what you learn in this book to students in third through twelfth grade, even though the activities are designed mainly for fourth through eighth graders. Remember that not every activity will work for your child. Use the ones that work, experiment, and adapt the information to fit your child's learning needs.

Before learning how to support your child as a learner, you as the parent need to understand:

1. What your child's responsibilities are in the learning process.

2. What constitutes learning.

3. What your child is like as a learner.

4. Methods and skills to improve your child's learning.

This book supports you in recognizing and understanding these criteria in relation to your child and provides workable answers to questions about learning.

Before moving on, it is important to understand the structure of this book and how following this structure benefits your child.

Book Structure

This book offers activities and strategies that focus on your child's preferred learning style. You will find over one hundred learning methods and skills that you can apply to your child's needs.

Homework strategies and corresponding activities help you apply your child's particular learning style to homework assignments. Feel free to choose only those activities you feel will increase your child's learning success.

The **chapters** in this book address learning and schoolwork problems. They also offer the reasoning behind the activities as well as their benefits and ways you can get the most out of them to help your child.

A **summary** of major points appears at the end of each chapter. These points give the reasoning behind each chapter's main focus.

You can complete the **activities** that follow each chapter summary with your child. Each activity includes goals, steps to complete the activity, and any challenges and opportunities the activity presents.

General Guidelines

While trying these activities, here are some guidelines to keep in mind that will greatly enhance your success in supporting your child as a learner:

1. There are no "bad" learning styles.
Each learning style has strengths and weaknesses. You will find ways to use your child's learning style to his or her best advantage.

2. Experiment.
The goal is to discover how your child can produce quality work and acquire meaningful learning more easily. If one approach fails, try another. You may need to customize each activity to your own child's needs.

3. Be patient and trust the learning process.
Every activity does not have to produce immediate results.

4. Take your time — learning often does.
There is a suggested amount of time for each activity, but this does not mean you can't go over the time allotted. Most children in fourth through eighth grade have a natural attention span of about ten minutes. If your child is still focused after ten minutes, stay with the activity. If not, just stop. You can come back to it later if you wish.

5. Celebrate your child's efforts.
Celebrating the effort your child puts into his or her work is important. A celebration can be simple and fun, like tossing confetti or using a special handshake. Remember to celebrate your child's efforts when completing the activities in this book, as well as in all homework assignments.

6. Have Fun.
Learning is pleasurable. Fun enhances learning, understanding, and memory. You will learn a lot about your child and yourself during the activities. Some of them may even become "games" that you and your child play when homework isn't the main focus.

Experiments in Learning

Try to view each of the activities and strategies as experiments. As in all legitimate experimentation, these learning experiments often involve a process of trial and error. This book can help speed up the process by suggesting methods and skills that work with your child's learning preference to produce a better learning experience.

The experiments may in themselves be valuable learning tools. Experimenting can reduce the difficulty of your tasks as you learn how to help your child become a lifelong learner.

Since human nature is complex and wildly variable, finding the "right answer" is often a matter of trying different approaches to see what works — and you determine what works.

Medical practitioners often use the same experimental approach when diagnosing your child. Because human health is also very complex, your doctor may send you home with a certain medicine and tell you to call in a couple of days to report whether it worked. You can do the same type of "experimenting" with your child's learning and homework. If one approach doesn't work, try another.

The learning strategies in this book focus on your child's homework. Many will prove to be effective immediately, becoming part of your child's learning skills. Experiment with the learning strategies and determine which work best for your child.

Whether it is helping with homework, all schoolwork, or even home schooling, this book offers proven methods for you to enhance and support your child's learning and academic success.

Summary:

- By using this book and taking The Kaleidoscope Profile® with your child, you will discover how to improve and support your child's learning.

- While supporting your child's learning, experiment, be patient, and have fun!

PART I

About Learning and Learning Styles

All parents have different ways of encouraging their children to do homework. Through experimentation, you have probably found that some ways work better than others. This book outlines many more ways to encourage your child to complete homework assignments successfully and without hassle.

Before you can expect your child to do homework well, you should both understand what learning is and how much responsibility you each have in the learning process. Once you read this book and apply the strategies, your child will put effort into and take responsibility for all assignments.

In order to learn, your child needs to retain, understand, and apply what is learned. These three components are discussed in detail in Part II, but they are introduced here to help define and lay a foundation for your child's learning.

Once you understand what learning is and what learning style your child uses according to The Kaleidoscope Profile®, you can better assist him or her with homework assignments. Your child will get the most from homework and make it easier and more enjoyable once these basics are in place.

The four learning styles or sensory preferences from The Kaleidoscope Profile® are also introduced and discussed in detail in Part I. These are:

- Visual: learns best by seeing, watching, reading.

- Auditory: learns by hearing, speaking, discussing, thinking aloud.

- Kinesthetic: learns while moving, doing things.

- Tactual: learns best by touch and feel, by relationship, emotion.

Once you can use your child's preferred learning style as a basis for all homework, encouraging him or her to complete assignments becomes easier.

Chapter 1

WHO IS RESPONSIBLE FOR THE LEARNING?

"The child who can begin early in life to see things as connected has begun the life of learning. The connectedness of things is what the educator contemplates."

— Dale Parnell, Author

The Kaleidoscope Profile®

Who is responsible for the learning? This is a question continually asked by parents, teachers, and students. While the question is raised frequently, the answer is unclear. What part of learning is your child's responsibility? The teacher's? Yours? It is important that people understand their roles in your child's learning.

The Adult's Responsibility

The adult (either the teacher or the parent) determines the range of an assignment and its difficulty for the child. In other words, the adult is responsible for how difficult or how easy any assignment is for the child.

Below is an equation for learning and academic success. This equation shows a breakdown of the different responsibilities in a child's learning process.

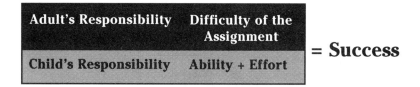

$$\frac{\text{Adult's Responsibility} \quad \text{Difficulty of the Assignment}}{\text{Child's Responsibility} \quad \text{Ability + Effort}} = \text{Success}$$

The Child's Responsibility

According to the equation above, your child brings two responsibilities to any assignment: his or her **ability** and his or her **effort**. Ability and effort put toward a homework assignment lead to learning success.

A poll of middle school students from around the world asked, "What produces success, ability or effort?" The vast majority of students said that effort is what produces success — except in the United States! The majority of students in the United States felt that ability was the key to success. What exactly are **ability** and **effort**, and how do they work?

Ability

Ability includes talent, learned skills, and learning style preference. Children have very little control over their ability. They either have the ability to do the task at the moment of learning or they don't.

The task of having to recite from memory provides a good example of the difference between ability and effort. If you were asked to recite the Gettysburg Address right now, you could either repeat it to some degree or you couldn't. There would be nothing you could do to increase your **ability** at this very moment. However, through **effort** you could learn the Gettysburg Address.

Effort

Teachers often grade for effort. Parents tell their children to "put some effort" into an assignment. However, few students in any grade could tell you what effort is or when they are making an effort to learn. For the purposes of this book, effort consists of three parts: **Practice**, **Repetition**, and **Perseverance**.

Practice is doing something in order to **improve performance** of skills in a particular activity. Filling out a check register or adding up miles between cities before taking an arithmetic test are examples of practice. Practice is meant to improve performance. Remember the saying, "Practice makes perfect."

Repetition is doing the **same thing over and over** again. Practicing one's tennis swing by repeatedly hitting a ball against a wall, reviewing for a test by reading the chapters it covers several times, or writing out spelling words ten times each to memorize for a quiz are all examples of repetition.

Note that practice and repetition might look the same. For the purposes of this book, the amount of effort (either skills development or memorization) for the improvement of a given activity indicates the difference between simple repetition and actual practice.

Perseverance is continued, patient practice and repetition. It is a learned behavior built on the belief that practice and/or repetition will increase one's ability to perform and succeed. As a parent, demonstrating your own belief in perseverance provides a powerful model for your child.

Perseverance is central to achievement and success.

The poll discussed above showed that many children in the United States do not see the relationship between effort and success. They believe success depends entirely on ability — either you've got it or you don't.

A true story further illustrates this belief. Natasha, a fourth-grade student, was placed in a math class that her teacher and parents knew would be a challenge for her. She felt intimidated by the "smarter kids" who seemed to understand the math assignments more quickly than she did. Her performance on the homework assignments discouraged her, and she scored poorly on the first two tests. The teacher realized that Natasha had already decided that she wouldn't do well in the class because she felt it was too advanced for her.

Natasha's teacher encouraged her parents to study with her for fifteen minutes a night for two weeks. When Natasha earned a passing grade on the next test, she thought she'd just been "lucky." But when the teacher asked each student to graph how much time he or she had spent studying in the last month, Natasha realized that there was a connection between her improved grade and the time she'd spent studying with her parents.

In an interview, Michael Jordan offered another good example of the relationship between effort and success. The interviewer asked, "Michael, how does it feel to completely blow away the opposition with your overwhelming talent?" Michael scoffed, "Talent? I've worked hard for my skills on the court. I worked years to perfect my moves. There are others with more talent than me, but if you don't see them out on the court beating me to the ball, it's because they don't work as hard as I do." Clearly Jordan felt that his continued repetition — his perseverance — led to his success, not just raw talent.

Thomas Edison also knew the value of effort. A newspaper reporter came to Edison after he had carried out more than 1,000 experiments trying to find a filament for the electric light bulb. The reporter asked Edison what it felt like to have failed 1,000 times. Edison replied, "Son, you don't understand how the world works. I'm 1,000 times closer to the discovery than anyone else." That opinion sums up what we want all children to believe about effort.

If your child makes the effort to learn, he or she will learn and will also increase his or her future ability. This ability leads to success, no matter how difficult the assignment may be. By helping your child understand how and why to practice, repeat, and persevere, you will help your child achieve great success.

Summary:

- Adults and children are both responsible for learning, but children are most accountable for bringing both their **ability** and **effort** to learning.

- Children are responsible for the effort they invest in the task of learning.

- Children will attempt any learning if they understand when and how practice, repetition, and perseverance are necessary.

Activity 1: Discussing Effort

Time: 10 minutes

Goals:

1. Gain a common understanding with your child of what effort is and why it's important.

2. Listen to your child's thoughts about effort.

Activity:

Sit down with your child and ask him or her to read one or more of the stories beginning on page 8: Natasha's math class, Michael Jordan's comments, and/or the Thomas Edison anecdote.

Then ask your child about his or her conclusions. Your question(s) could be phrased as follows:

- "What did you think of the stories?"

- "What do you think of Thomas Edison's idea about how the world works?"

- "What do you feel is the connection between effort and doing well at school?"

- "What do you think effort is?"

- "Does your teacher grade on effort?"

- "Sometimes when a student gets a good grade on a test, classmates respond by saying, 'You're so lucky!' How much luck do you think is involved in doing well in school?"

Accept the answers as information, rather than attitudes or beliefs that need to be corrected during the activity. Share with your daughter or son the definition and components of effort in this book: remember to use Practice, Repetition, and Perseverance (see pages 7-8).

Follow up the discussion later by pointing out to your child whenever he or she is making an effort (using practice, repetition, or perseverance) with the homework or any learning.

Mention some examples of effort and success from past homework/schoolwork experiences that your child has had. Above all, continually show your child the connection between effort and his or her success in and out of school.

Challenges:

How often have you sat with your child to talk about school when you haven't been addressing a problem? If schoolwork has been a problem in the past, your child will probably think that this discussion is about a problem too.

You may have to spend time reassuring your child that this discussion about effort is different. You can demonstrate its difference by ending the discussion without making an evaluation of any kind or offering any comments about the conversation. This approach may feel different to your child and can set a new tone for future conversations as well as for doing the activities in this book.

Opportunities:

You may be starting something new with these discussions about effort, or you may be reinforcing something you have done before with your child. Either way, you are opening a "learning dialogue" between the two of you. In the learning dialogue there are no "right" answers. Instead, you will be acquiring new information about how your child learns.

Completing this activity can be a powerful experience. It may feel strange at first, but it will produce new behaviors in your child. And you will have an opportunity to enjoy another side of your daughter or son. The opportunity lies in your consistent commitment to having these types of daily conversations about school with your child. Ask questions about school and daily events (whether special or routine), and seek out your child's opinions *without judgment* during the conversation.

Your child depends on you to help increase his or her odds of learning quickly and efficiently. Make it too hard, and your child will give up. Make it too easy, and he or she will lose interest. That is the art of balancing the difficulty of the assignment with the effort your child puts in. Through trial and error, you will find a happy medium.

Setting learning goals for your child and not changing them shows that you have faith in his or her ability to achieve those goals. Being flexible with the ways to learn tells your child that he or she can control the conditions of learning and ensure success.

The main purpose of this book is to provide you with numerous methods for varying the difficulty of a task by using what is known about learning styles. Your responsibility to your child's learning and the effort he or she puts forth is to increase success by moderating the difficulty of the task.

Activity 2: Tackling Difficult Work
Time: 10 minutes

Goals:

1. Build your child's confidence through brainstorming and open inquiry.

2. Listen to your child.

3. Practice the responsibilities of learning (effort and ability).

4. Find out what obstacles hinder your child's understanding of homework assignments.

Activity:

Start a discussion concerning what your child thinks is difficult about a given homework assignment and what is easy. You should get a sense of your child's emotional reactions to "not understanding." At the same time you will increase your own knowledge about how he or she completes assignments. What you discover could be valuable in later activities.

To discover how your child feels, you will need to open a nonconfrontational dialogue. To do this, ask open questions that allow your child to provide as much detail as possible. It's also important that your child doesn't feel defensive or that you are accusing him or her of doing something wrong. Asking something like, "What do you feel you know about the multiplication problem?" will inspire a fuller explanation than asking, "Do you understand this?" The first question invites an explanation, while the second invites only a "yes" or "no" answer.

Here is an example of a possible conversation:

- Child: I don't understand fractions.

- Parent: How do you know you don't?

- Child: I don't know what to do (or) I keep getting the wrong answers (or) I don't know what the teacher wants.

- Parent: Well, show me what you have done. Perhaps if you explain it to me, it will be easier for you to understand. What parts are easy? (or) Show me what you do understand of the assignment.

By having a conversation similar to this one, your child will be encouraged to take the responsibility for his or her learning and is challenged to tackle the assignment with your encouragement and support.

Sometimes children can become discouraged or give up due to frustration. Take the time to help your child explore exactly what he or she doesn't understand by asking open questions. By helping to break an assignment into steps, your child may realize that he or she actually knows a lot about it. The whole assignment may become less difficult when your child feels more confident.

For added encouragement, review practice, repetition, and perseverance (pages 7-8) with your child. Use examples of past successes to boost your child's confidence.

Challenges:

This is a problem solving activity. Your role is that of the teacher. You are working together instead of having your child simply recite your responses. This process takes patience. It may not be something your child has ever done. Remember that effort takes practice and perseverance from both you and your child.

Opportunities:

In this activity and while you and your child confront difficult assignments, you have an opportunity to model patience, optimism concerning success, and confidence in your child's ability to think. You need to be confident of your child's success before there is any evidence that you should be, and certainly before your child is.

Consider this a brainstorming activity or a "what do you think?" process where you are gaining information about how your child works. You and your child may not generate any "right" answers at all; you may find that you simply make a list of questions for your child to ask the teacher the next day. In any case, you will learn more about how your child thinks and learns, and your child will feel comfortable coming to you for support with homework problems.

Remember that when your child has successes, celebrate them with a cheer or a special handshake. Little reinforcements can mean a lot to your child's confidence.

Chapter 2

LEARNING: WHAT IS IT?

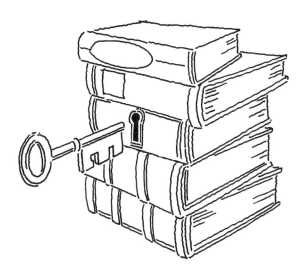

"Parents and teachers constantly talk about getting kids to learn. However, they rarely agree on what 'learning' means."

— William Haggart, Educator and Author

The Kaleidoscope Profile®

What does *to learn* mean? The answer is not obvious, but by understanding the meaning of *to learn*, you will understand what your child is trying to accomplish in school.

When over 2,000 middle and high school students in five states responded to the question "What does *to learn* mean?" the majority said that learning is "remembering what the teacher says." It is doubtful that any teacher or parent would be happy with that definition.

A working definition of learning is necessary in helping your child improve his or her learning process.

**The definition of learning
includes three parts:**

1. Retention

2. Understanding

3. Application

Below is a breakdown of each part in greater detail.

1. Retention
Retention includes memorizing information and being able to recall this information when necessary. No real learning takes place if a child simply forgets what was taught.

The learning style preference plays a powerful role in how easily and effectively your child can memorize information. Beginning on page 75, you will find suggestions for improving your child's memorization skills. Each suggestion is applied to a particular preference.

Figure 1 shows what learning style teaching methods are most and least effective for helping students retain what they are taught.

The Learning Triangle

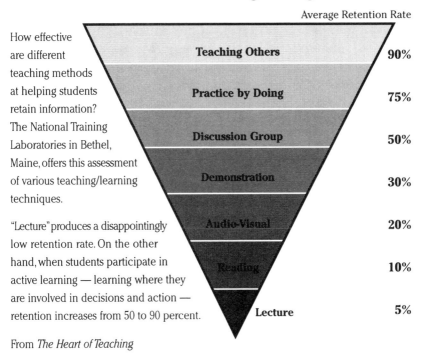

Average Retention Rate

How effective are different teaching methods at helping students retain information? The National Training Laboratories in Bethel, Maine, offers this assessment of various teaching/learning techniques.

"Lecture" produces a disappointingly low retention rate. On the other hand, when students participate in active learning — learning where they are involved in decisions and action — retention increases from 50 to 90 percent.

Teaching Others	90%
Practice by Doing	75%
Discussion Group	50%
Demonstration	30%
Audio-Visual	20%
Reading	10%
Lecture	5%

From *The Heart of Teaching*

Figure 1: The Learning Triangle

2. Understanding

Understanding is the ability to see how things are connected and related. Often intelligence or creativity is defined as a person's ability to see similarities and connections where most people cannot. For example, memorizing the Gettysburg Address is a matter of simple recall, while understanding the Gettysburg Address is knowing what it means and why it's important.

Students need to remember simple information such as $2 + 2 = 4$. They also need to understand the concepts behind the equation, what makes it true, and how to add. Perhaps your child has memorized the steps needed for solving problems in long division, but if he or she doesn't know that division is a process of separating objects into groups of equal size or number, there is a lack of understanding.

Understanding is based on experience and information. A child can read about flying an airplane, but the experience of sitting in the pilot's seat provides an understanding that books can't give. Similarly, when children "play," most of their activities involve finding connections between concepts, toys, and each other. As Albert Einstein once said, "Play is the highest form of research." For children, play leads to understanding.

> *Children set no time limits on their efforts to understand, even if they feel an urgency to know.*

It's just as well, because achieving understanding is very difficult to time. Most of us have had an "aha!" experience in which we finally grasp something after a long period of simply "not getting it." That is understanding.

Understanding does not receive enough attention in school, probably because achieving it requires an unpredictable amount of time. Homework can provide some of the additional time often needed for true understanding of school subjects.

3. Application

Learning is ultimately useless if it can't be applied in some manner. The world is changing quickly — new problems and opportunities are created every day. It's becoming increasingly difficult to predict how students will be asked to apply their learning later in the workplace or in other aspects of their lives. Because of this, your child needs to know how to apply what he or she has learned in a wide variety of ways.

Homework can provide many varied opportunities for applying knowledge. For example, arithmetic homework can offer problems involving spending money, cooking for large or small numbers of people, and figuring mileage for a trip.

The ability to apply knowledge, like the ability to understand it, enables your child to solve unfamiliar problems.

Of course, these three parts of learning (retention, understanding, and application) are connected. Figure 2 shows how they work. Understanding increases retention, and application can deepen understanding. In this book, learning is separated into three parts for ease of understanding and application.

The Learning Process

The Ingredients of Retention	The Ingredients of Understanding	The Ingredients of Application
• Three or more repetitions of the information. • Meaningful and useful information. • Tricks for increasing the likelihood of remembering something, like Roy G Biv for the colors of the rainbow.	• The opportunity to practice skills and information without grading or judgment. • Three or more experiences of the same information. • A variety of examples to allow for comparison or contrast.	• Using skills in a real situation. • Creating a project using prior learning.

The three parts of learning work together and support each other. For example, the elements of understanding provide the repetition for information needed for retention.

Figure 2: The Learning Process

Summary:

• Learning has three parts:

  o **Retention** (recalling what is learned)

  o **Understanding** (knowing what is learned)

  o **Application** (using what is learned)

• These descriptions of learning are valuable tools for increasing your child's learning success.

| Activity 3: Learning and Teaching |
| Time: 5 - 10 minutes |

Goals:

1. Encourage your child to retain a lesson through the experience of "teaching" it.

2. Use sharing and comparing to learn and teach homework assignments.

Activity:

You have seen your child work to understand homework assignments. Encouraging your child to learn and teach can become part of homework. Here are some ways your child can try learning and teaching:

- **Comparing**
  Sometimes your child has learned a concept differently from how you learned it in school (e.g., math procedures, such as dividing fractions; or terms in English, such as the parts of speech or the parts of an essay).

  Have your child show you how he or she has learned division, and then you show your child how you were taught. Don't judge or tell your child which is the "better" way to do division. Just emphasize the comparison.

- **Sibling Sharing**

  If you have two children, the older might be willing to teach the younger sibling something new that the older child is learning. In this case the "teaching" child is actually enhancing his or her own learning. The younger child is often just thrilled to be learning something the "big kids" are learning, as well as getting some attention from big sister or brother.

- **Teaching the Parent**

  At times your child will be excited about something he or she has learned in school. Encourage your child to tell you all about it.

  One parent used this activity when his child came home fascinated by wolves. The child told his dad everything he had learned about wolves and how they lived. Since he was explaining something new that his father didn't know about, he became increasingly eager to offer more information. The activity also enhanced the child's retention of the information.

Notice what you see and hear during this learning and teaching activity. Your child may become very excited to teach you, and may do additional research to find answers to any questions you have about the subject matter. Using a variety of homework assignments, have your child "teach" you in as many of the following ways as possible and note when:

- Your child explains something in different ways to help you understand.

- Your child thinks of an example or a likeness to help you understand.

- Your child goes back to the beginning of an explanation or procedure when you don't seem to understand.

- Your child shows patience in explaining a procedure or concept.

- Your child offers encouragement to you.

Challenges:

If your child thinks that the purpose of homework is to get it done as soon as possible rather than learning from it, you may find resistance to any idea of trying something new or different, such as teaching you or a sibling. Doing something new may require more time for your child. In order to do this activity, it may be better to find a school assignment or subject that your child actually enjoys or use an assignment your child has to learn but is having trouble with. Academic homework tends to work better in a teaching situation than art or other kinds of projects since most academic homework requires learning facts and information that can be easily shared.

A child may feel uncomfortable instructing his or her parent but enjoy teaching a younger sibling or a grandparent. Again, participating in a teaching and learning situation may be something that the family has to grow into rather than accomplish in one evening.

Opportunities:

This learning and teaching activity offers new ways of doing homework and building relationships among family members. If your child finds it useful for doing homework or just enjoys the attention and company, it could become a family activity — which is a plus in itself.

You'll also have a much better idea of what's happening with schoolwork if you're involved with your child's homework assignments.

Activity 4: Discussing the Three Parts of Learning
Time: 10 minutes

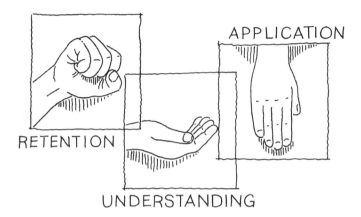

RETENTION

APPLICATION

UNDERSTANDING

Goals:

1. Teach your child the three parts of learning (retention, understanding, and application).
2. Understand how the three parts of learning apply to homework assignments.

Activity:

Review the three parts of learning — retention, understanding, and application beginning on page 18 — with your child. You might start out by asking "Have you ever wondered what *learning* means?"

Have your child repeat the three parts with you while matching your hand motions:

- Retention (make a tight fist).

- Understanding (hold one hand open, palm up).

- Application (bring the palm down on a flat surface).

Using the hand motions can help reinforce the components of learning, so go through them with your child at least three times.

Make up an exercise that applies the three different parts of learning to your child's homework. For example, if your child is learning to add, make up an exercise that uses Popsicle sticks. Have your child grasp two sticks in his or her fist. Place two more sticks in his or her fist to illustrate 2 + 2 = 4. Physical activity aids **retention**. Using tangible physical objects like Popsicle sticks rather than abstractions like numbers written on a page helps **understanding**. Using the principles of addition to add up groups of other objects, such as coins or poker chips, demonstrates the use of **application**.

Have your child identify each of the three different parts of learning in the exercise you made up. Be sure he or she uses the hand motions for each part. Talk about how each one helps your child learn the lesson of the homework.

Don't worry about total accuracy in the homework at this point. Go for a deeper understanding. Note any "ahas" you and your child might have about the objectives of the homework, as well as questions. Have your child do the hand motions for retention, understanding, and application for many different assignments, even if the actions seem exaggerated or silly.

Challenges:

This is an instructional activity in which you are the teacher introducing new information as you present the three parts of learning: retention, understanding, and application. No "right" answers are required. You may feel awkward teaching something that you don't feel you yourself fully understand. Don't worry — it's fine if you and your child are participating in this learning together.

Remember a time when you taught your child skills that did not pertain to school, such as how to mow the lawn or pitch a tent. Your "teaching" abilities from that time can transfer to this activity. You can even discuss how retention, understanding, and application helped your child to learn those skills.

Opportunities:

While your child experiences the three parts of learning as they apply to various assignments, you may find that related topics about school come up. These might include your child's feelings about school and homework, how your child relates to his or her teacher(s), and why some subjects are easier to understand than others. You may want to take several opportunities to carry out this teaching activity because of all the things you will both learn.

Activity 5: Homework Purposes

Time: 15 minutes

Goals:

1. Determine the purpose (retention, understanding, or application) of a homework assignment.

2. Increase your child's focus and sense of clarity regarding homework assignments.

3. Enhance your child's confidence that he or she can do the homework successfully.

4. (Optional) Meet with your child's teacher to clarify the purposes of homework assignments for you and your child. Knowing the goals of the homework should make doing the homework that much more successful.

Activity:

Any evening when your child has homework, ask him or her to tell you about the assignments. Using Figure 3, sit down together and determine the purpose(s) of each assignment. Decide first what kind of assignment it is, matching it with a category in the vertical column on the left, (e.g., "Reading to Answer Questions"). Then decide whether the purpose of the assignment is retention, understanding, or application. Note how this new knowledge increases your child's focus and sense of clarity, and enhances his or her self-confidence.

Learning and the Types of Homework

	Retention	Understanding	Application
Solving Problems/ Practicing Skills A series of questions or problems. Examples: math problems or sentences to diagram.	Memory is improved through sheer repetition of several problems or tasks of the same kind.	Understanding can be enhanced by repeating a task when the common parts of the task (e.g., addition) are identified and used in several problems.	If the skills/ knowledge will be used in real life, then this type of homework is an application of skills.
Reading to Answer Questions Reading in order to comprehend information in history, social studies, science, or language arts.	Retention can occur if there are some "memory hooks" to help with the reading. Retention is not a major education objective of a reading assignment.	Having to answer questions requires understanding the meaning of what is read.	Unless there are skills used in the task of comprehension, this is not an application assignment.
Projects and Reports Something is made, built, or written. It can involve a one-night assignment or a long-term assignment worked on over several weeks.	While these assignments can be memorable, doing them is not primarily meant to increase retention.	The process of making, building, or writing enhances understanding.	Application is the primary purpose of these kinds of assignments: What can the student do with skills and knowledge — often the ability to find data is also important.

Figure 3: Learning and the Types of Homework

Learning and the Types of Homework

	Retention	Understanding	Application
Study Memorization or preparing for tests. Can be practicing a skill or testing understanding.	This is where the variety of memorization skills comes into play. To study is primarily to memorize, and secondarily to check for understanding.	Studying for understanding means to review in order to identify what is/is not understood in prep-aration for a test or performance (essay, speech).	There is very little application possi-ble when studying, unless the assign-ment is to use "study skills."
Creative Assignments Writing stories, doing projects, completing art assignments.	Again, these assignments can be memorable, but are not designed to help students memorize.	Any creative assignment will increase under-standing because it requires students to compare and contrast in new ways.	In creative assign-ments, learned skills and knowl-edge are applied in new ways. These assignments offer an important way to allow for appli-cation while enhancing understanding.

Figure 3: Learning and the Types of Homework

Challenges:

Your child's teacher may have reasons for a given homework assignment that differ from those in Figure 3. If you have questions about the purpose of your child's homework, you can ask them in a note to the teacher or arrange a meeting. You can talk to the teacher at the meeting about your efforts to teach your child to recognize the "why" of homework assignments. This meeting should be an effort at teamwork rather than a challenge to the teacher's curriculum or homework assignments.

Your child can have reasons for doing the homework that don't necessarily match the teacher's purpose. It may be that your child knows he or she needs to understand the math problems, while the homework was assigned as a retention activity. Focusing your child's efforts on developing his or her skills is the most important aspect of this activity.

Opportunities:

Analyzing the purposes of a homework assignment is an analytical skill that your child can use through college and beyond. Coming to conclusions based on analysis is a vital thinking process that takes time to learn. Using this activity to make schoolwork easier, more meaningful, and more productive is also a powerful lesson for your child.

Since this is a thought-intensive exercise, be sure to celebrate your child's efforts.

Chapter 3

LEARNING STYLES

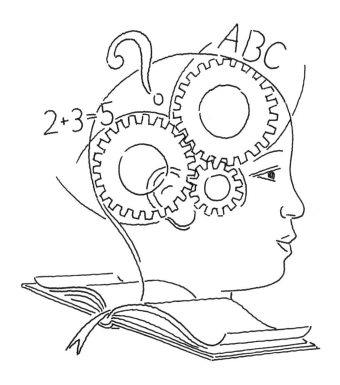

"As we come to understand more about learning and teaching styles and how the mind operates, I believe we will improve mental health and self-understanding as well as increase learning."

— Anthony F. Gregorc, Educator and Author

Even though all children learn in the same way — through retention, understanding, and application — each child approaches an assignment in his or her own style. This chapter helps you to understand your child's style: her or his own set of strengths and needs regarding the task of learning. Style is not a measure of intelligence or ability, but a set of likes and dislikes that affects your child's approach to learning.

Your child favors one or more of the senses in learning through retention, understanding, and application of information and skills.

Sensory Styles

Figure 4 outlines the sensory preferences your child can use to learn. As a parent, you are probably already aware of your child's style in a number of areas.

A Description of Sensory Learning Preferences

Kinesthetic Learner	Tactual Learner	Auditory Learner	Visual Learner
Active Learner	Feeling Learner	Conversational Learner	Observant Learner
Wants to move and do things with whole body to gain information and learn. Wants to make things work to understand them.	Prefers to learn through small muscle movement (such as touch), feeling the environment, and emotional responses. Wants to sense how things work.	Experiences learning by talking and listening. Needs to hear, speak, discuss, and think out loud to learn. Wants to talk about how things work.	Wants to see, watch, read, and view to learn. Wants to "see" how things work.

Figure 4: A Brief Description of Sensory Learning Preferences

The primary way people experience the world is through the senses. Everything we learn enters our awareness through the senses. Your body takes in over 50,000 sensory impressions per second — everything from the pressure of this book in your hand to the temperature in the room and the noise next door. You can't possibly remain conscious of all these sensory impressions, so your body and mind pick "favorites."

Whichever sense or combination of senses your brain chooses affects how you learn or determines how you will learn most efficiently. This is called the **body connection** to learning.

The first contact with any new knowledge or skill comes through the body's senses.

Sensory preferences are distributed throughout the general population as follows:

- 30% Kinesthetic (body movement and physical handling to determine how something works)

- 20% Tactual (touching to determine how something feels, smelling, tasting)

- 15% Auditory (hearing, listening, and discussing)

- 35% Visual (seeing physically and visualizing)

The chart on pages 36-37 outlines the traits associated with the four sensory preferences. You will probably recognize that many of the traits correspond to your child's learning strengths and difficulties, as well as to your own.

Learning Traits, Preferences, and Difficulties

Type	Traits	Preferences	Difficulties
Kinesthetic "Doer"	Learns by being physically involved in learning. Looks for challenges and exciting projects. Likes creating learning "products" such as flash cards. Learning characterized by large movements and energy.	Experiments and learns through trial and error. Seeks understanding through physical activity. Uses action as a way of gathering information and learning. Moves and physically examines things and problems. Limited physical activity (e.g., foot tapping) can help concentration rather than distract from it.	Sitting still for long periods of time — especially if asked to learn. Recalling what is seen or heard. Expressing self without physical movement and gestures. Staying with an activity for long periods of time without a break. Doing detailed work, which might include writing or working with small objects.
Tactual "Feeler"	Learns through touch and emotion. Easily occupied by smaller, more refined physical movements, often taking pleasure in detailed work. Can be considered sensitive because environmental physical conditions such as heat and cold or the emotional atmosphere of a room can help or hinder learning.	Learns the "people connections" to things, such as learning about Abraham Lincoln in relation to the Gettysburg Address. Does projects that involve self-expression and work he or she finds appealing. Learns by instinctive leaps, rather than through step-by-step processes. Finds own unique way of learning, doing homework, or doing anything else.	Learning alone or in uninteresting environments. Working with teachers or other students he or she does not like. Learning without being able to touch, express feelings, or manipulate things. Learning abstract facts.
Visual "Observer"	Learns by looking at and seeing what he or she needs to know. Appreciates first watching others do what he or she will be asked to learn. Tends to watch and gather information before taking action in learning.	Visualizes problems and solutions by picturing them in the mind. Wants time to quietly observe or read while learning. Enjoys research as part of the learning process. Creates visual diagrams, pictures, and lists.	Listening and remembering verbal information. Expressing himself or herself verbally. Working in a visually overstimulating or visually drab environment. Learning in an environment with lots of noise or activity.

Figure 5: Learning Traits, Preferences, and Difficulties

Learning Traits, Preferences, and Difficulties

Type	Traits	Preferences	Difficulties
Auditory "Talker"	Learns through discussion, listening, and speaking. Sounds of all kinds play a major role in learning. Tells you what he or she is doing and invites sharing as a way to learn.	Works and learns using words and language. Enjoys pleasant, harmonious sounds in the learning environment. Likes having others around to talk to during the learning experience. Responds well when new information or skills are explained.	Reading without talking aloud to himself or herself or reading silently for long periods of time. Learning visual information or physical skills without explanation. Following written directions or taking written tests. Identifying important visual information, such as diagrams or pictures.

Figure 5: Learning Traits, Preferences, and Difficulties

Each learner will use other approaches to learning only when the first, preference-related attempt has failed.

For example, consider how different individuals behave when they are driving to a new place and need directions. Some will stop at a gas station and ask to see a map — the visual preference. They don't want to be told how to reach their destination because they learn best when they can look at the route on a map and visualize it in their minds after they drive away. They also know they have a hard time remembering spoken directions.

Others will prefer that the station attendant tell them the directions — the auditory preference. They will "hear" the directions in their minds and be able to follow them later. These learners can remember even complex verbal instructions but can have difficulty interpreting a map of the area.

Kinesthetic learners learn by doing, so they would probably pass the gas station by and drive around, hunting out their destination by trial and error.

Tactual learners often won't stop either, unless others in the car want to. Instead they will rely on their sense of direction, knowing where they are at the moment in relation to where they are going. For instance, they may be aware of which way is north or remember a description of the area rather than the directions to it. They are also more likely to canvas other people in the car for their ideas instead of stopping at a gas station.

People usually make such decisions subconsciously because they're accustomed to relying on their sensory preference.

Your child approaches learning in much the same way, leading with the sense he or she prefers and has experienced the most success with: observing, talking, doing, or feeling.

> *By using it repeatedly, your child has become more skilled in his or her preferred sense than in the other senses.*

Applying your child's preference to homework is helpful in developing a deeper understanding of how your child learns. The activities that follow involve some of the dynamics of learning styles at home and at school. They provide a number of techniques and ideas you can use when working with your child or communicating with school staff.

Summary:

- Understanding his or her learning style can help your child focus on improving homework.

- The Kaleidoscope Profile® is a fun way to identify your child's learning preference as well as your own through hands-on, personal interaction. To find out more about it, see page v.

Activity 6: Learning Styles at Home

Time: 15 minutes

Goals:

1. Identify what learning styles you and your child use at home.

2. Provide an initial discussion of learning styles in an exploratory, nonjudgmental fashion.

3. Increase mutual understanding by comparing learning styles in a positive way.

Activity:

Read through the descriptions on the chart located on the next page, noting the ones that seem to fit your child. Other related behaviors not listed on the chart may also come to mind as you read.

Sit down with your child and share this chart. Ask in a nonjudgmental way if he or she recognizes any of the behaviors. Perhaps just say, "I have something here that shows how we behave at home. Which behaviors are like you?"

Sensory Preferences/Common Home Behaviors					
	Favorite Place and Activity	**Behaviors at Play**	**Behaviors during Chores/Room Cleaning**	**Types of Misbehavior**	**Responses to Family Activities**
Kinesthetic "Doer"	Does physical activities with friends. Enjoys projects and games. Plays outside.	Makes loud noise. Very active in games, exploring. Builds forts, tree houses.	Cleans room too quickly and poorly. Often needs chore reminders. Hard worker when challenged.	Tardiness. Tests limits physically. Outbursts rather than discussion.	Loves outings and sports. Family time sometimes secondary to physical activity and outdoor play.
Tactual "Feeler"	Personalizes room and favorite hideouts. Likes a few favorite people. Loves animals and has "causes."	Often expresses emotions in or about play. Prefers social activities with friends where "atmosphere" is important.	Fusses over detail. Wants to do chores with others. Emphasizes comfort in the physical environment.	Any punishment is taken personally. Personal ideas of what is "right" justify misbehavior. Can be overly emotional about issues.	Wants family harmony and activities. Enjoys doing things together. Can have high expectations.
Visual "Observer"	Likes to be alone and "watch." Spends time in room and quiet places. Creates things to look at or show.	Very quiet in play. Sets up scenes with toys and builds for "looks." Spends a lot of time "getting it right."	Concerned over how things look. Wants things neat. Has to "see" what needs to be done.	Passive/aggressive misbehavior such as avoidance or "silent treatment." Silence. Visual cues of anger/disrespect.	Wants to think about any plans. Tends to want to be invited. Will seldom initiate plans for family activities.
Auditory "Talker"	Seldom alone in play. Enjoys being with lots of people.	Lots of talking and dialogue in play. Often involved in social play like "tea party" or "playing school."	Needs to talk about work before and during chores. Follows directions.	Talks back or tries to talk way out of problems.	Wants family discussion and planning. Enjoys family reminiscing.

Figure 6: Sensory Preferences and Common Home Behaviors

The behavioral comparisons on the chart are sure to produce some recognition of behaviors that are typical of your child.

Without saying which behaviors you think are characteristic, let your child explain why he or she has chosen particular ones. If there are differences between your views and your child's, consider them valuable information. You should also be prepared to share your responses to the chart regarding your own behaviors.

Challenges:

Since identifying learning styles requires personal sharing, revealing feelings, and making personal choices, this activity can be difficult for your child. Your child may feel that you have expectations that he or she may want to meet rather than responding honestly. Be prepared to answer any number of questions from your child about why you are doing this particular activity. Let your child know that there aren't any "wrong" or "bad" answers.

Using a curious but unconcerned approach will help defuse these possible anxieties. The activity is meant to provide a non-academic way of considering learning styles, but any meaningful discussion can bring up personal issues, so be prepared. The discussion could also bring up family routines, choices, and even family history. Deflecting such issues or following up is your choice.

Opportunities:

The opportunity in this assignment is to talk about important issues involving school and family while discussing learning styles in a nonthreatening way.

One of the most important topics that can arise in the discussion is your child's view of his or her "place" in your family. Your child might see other family members in the descriptions and gain new understanding by comparing and contrasting different styles. This activity can yield powerful learning time and strengthen your child's bond with your family.

Chapter 4

DOES HOMEWORK HAVE TO BE A BATTLE?

"I can't do it. It's too hard."
"I'll do it later."
"Why do I need to learn this anyway?"

— Some typical reactions when children
were asked to do their homework

The Kaleidoscope Profile®

This chapter applies to all types of schoolwork but focuses on the one you can influence the most: homework. Homework is a controversial issue. Some believe that students need to do more, while others feel that all homework is a waste of time.

Most studies show that student success is linked to the amount of homework students are assigned. In other words:

Increased homework means increased student achievement.

Homework assignments encourage the repetition and practice of skills that the time constraints of a regular school day don't permit. Homework allows time for individual study, projects, and learning that are not possible during school hours. Students can use homework to build work and study skills, to memorize, and to prepare for tests and assignments.

Ten minutes of homework per grade, starting in the second grade, is reasonable. Homework should be assigned every weeknight but Friday. That means that a sixth grader would have fifty minutes of homework a night, four nights a week. A ninth grader would have an hour and twenty minutes of homework a night, with possible longer assignments to do over the weekend. This is a rule of thumb that many schools follow.

If you feel that the amount of homework assigned to your child is excessive and way beyond the ten minutes per grade rule of thumb, here are some suggestions to keep homework from being such a battle for you:

1. Talk to your child's teacher. State your concerns and ask why so much homework is given. Perhaps the teacher isn't aware that the assignments are taking a large amount of time. This is often true when several teachers assign homework without coordinating how much each is assigning.

2. If the teacher doesn't offer to work with you to reduce the amount of homework, don't argue. Instead, discuss your concern with other parents. The teacher may feel uncomfortable about reducing the amount of homework for reasons that you don't know and that he or she is unable to discuss. The reason may even be that other parents have asked for more homework.

3. Ask the principal or school superintendent what results are expected from the amount of homework assigned. These individuals may or may not be able to answer your question, but at least you have initiated a discussion. If someone does provide a satisfactory explanation, ask if the results can be or have been achieved without such large amounts of homework. If the answer is yes, or if no one knows the answer, you have a good reason to ask for a change.

4. If none of these suggestions produces a satisfactory conclusion, then go to the school board, explaining what you have found out and why you are asking them to help. Some teachers and other parents will probably be interested in the issue too. Above all, be reasonable, but persistent. It is possible that no one — neither the school board, site council, teachers, parents, nor the administration — will act on the issue. If this is true, you probably aren't going to change the homework policy, as school districts are representative organizations. See if you can find teachers at your child's school who will work with you, or find another school for your child to attend if you feel the issue is that important.

By bringing up issues that no one else is aware of, you may be successful just by talking with a teacher or someone in the school administration. It's also possible, however, that your child is having difficulties with homework for reasons that have nothing to do with how much has been assigned.

For many students homework often feels like "busy work," they want to "just get done." Sometimes they might be right about this. In both public and private schools it can be difficult to predict what educators will cite as reasons for homework assignments. There are many rationales for homework, including keeping students off the streets or making parents happy.

> ***When your child asks, "Why do I have to do homework?" you have to be prepared to answer.***

Here are some ways you can help your child answer that question.

Discuss homework with the family

As a parent, you can fill a number of roles that are important to your child's success with homework. The first is to come to some family conclusions about the purposes of homework.

Some families refer to all schoolwork as their children's "jobs," because children learn how to work while doing it. Have a family discussion about the purposes of homework, and determine the role it plays in your home.

Discuss homework with teachers

Second, talk to your child's teachers about their specific expectations and the purposes they have in mind for the homework they assign. Teachers are often frustrated with the quality of the homework they get from their students. If they are clear about their expectations when they assign the homework, they will find it far easier to achieve their purposes.

Discuss homework with your child

Third, work with your child to identify the purpose (retention, understanding, or application) of each homework assignment. Go over the benefits of homework that is done well. Children need to see the immediate cause and effect of their actions to learn well.

Human beings are designed to learn and desire to succeed. Your child wants to succeed in school, even when his or her efforts seem to contradict this. Once your child has some success with homework assignments, he or she will want more success. Remember that encouraging your child's efforts will eventually lead to success.

Powerful Learning Experiences

Do you remember a school assignment that intrigued you and fired your imagination? A sixth grader named Carlos became so engrossed in a science report that he did far more work than required. He demonstrated a drive wholly unrelated to school grades. He spent eight hours pecking out the report on a computer on a Saturday, even though he hated typing and the assignment wasn't due for over a week. This was not his normal behavior when it came to homework. Usually completing any assignment turned into a battle of wills between Carlos and his mother.

When his mother mentioned how hard Carlos had worked on the assignment, he was confused. In his mind hard work was something unpleasant that required perseverance.

Carlos had a powerful learning experience. He could have received a 100 percent on the assignment by doing only half the work he had done. Having a child that dedicated to an assignment is the ultimate goal of every teaching method and every effort to support students in doing homework. Powerful learning is hard work, but it is rarely unpleasant.

Your experiments with homework and learning make your child capable of experiencing dedication as part of his or her learning.

Acknowledge your child's successful efforts to complete homework with brief celebrations, such as high fives or a short cheer. There is value in rewarding your child's positive behavior rather than focusing on the grade or the outcome of assignments. If your child has studied extensively but hasn't received a grade commensurate with the time put in, reward your child for the time investment. Eventually the grade will improve if you maintain positive reinforcement.

Summary:

- The unchanging requirement of homework is that quality work be produced. How it is accomplished can and should vary widely to accommodate all learners.

Activity 7: Determining the Purposes of Homework

Time: 10 minutes

Goals:

1. Determine your attitudes about homework and how they can influence your child.

2. Emphasize the importance of homework to your child.

Activity:

This activity prepares you for your child's question, "Why do I have to do homework?" Your preparation for and response to this question can influence your child's approach to homework assignments.

Write out a list of reasons why you think doing homework is worthwhile. For instance, you may tell your child that the homework is his or her "job," just as you have a job that you go to. This gives your child a reference and a comparison for his or her effort.

Perhaps your child has expressed interest in being a zookeeper. You could emphasize the importance of science to understand how the animals think, and math to calculate how many pounds of hay to order for the elephant each year. Figuring out how school subjects pertain to your child's hopes for the future can be excellent motivation. Even as your child's interests change, you can always find a way to link a school subject with his or her chosen career.

The key to this activity is to be clear and consistent about the reasons your child needs to do homework.

Challenges:

It may be difficult to come up with compelling reasons for why your child must do homework. You have probably formulated some of your own as you have read this chapter. You may wish to compile and share a list of your own reasons. Your child may find the reasons motivational too.

Opportunities:

This is an excellent opportunity to discuss the question, "Why do I have to do homework?" Many parents simply respond, "To get good grades" or "So you can get into college." However, these reasons may not be good enough for your child. You can refer to the list of reasons doing homework is worthwhile, and perhaps you and your child can add to this list during this discussion.

Activity 8: Powerful Learning Experiences
Time: 30 minutes

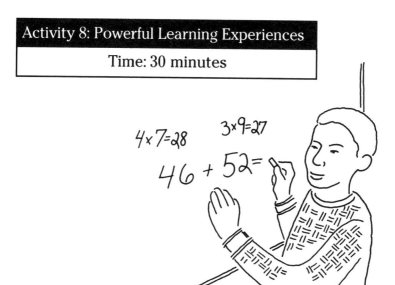

Goals:

1. Determine what powerful learning experiences your child has had.

2. Decide why those experiences are memorable for your child.

Activity:

Tell your child the story about Carlos (see page 49) or a similar experience that you have had. Ask your child if he or she can remember having had such an experience too. If your child can recall one, you might write down some of the things that made it such a powerful learning experience for him or her. You can use this information in later activities.

Here are some sample questions to ask about your child's powerful learning experience(s):

- What did you find interesting about what you learned in the assignment?

- Was the assignment like anything you'd done before? What made it similar or different?

- What did you make or do for the assignment? Do you usually like assignments that have the same requirements? Was this assignment different from the ones you usually get?

- Did you find any part of the assignment difficult? Why or why not?

- What kinds of schoolwork do you find are similar to that learning experience?

Be sure to celebrate the effort it took to consider the questions in this activity.

Challenges:

Discussing powerful learning experiences may feel alien to your child. Because children are often taught that unpleasant schoolwork is "learning," and anything pleasant or engaging is "fun" but not "learning," they may find it difficult to recollect a time when they experienced powerful learning.

Your child may find it easier to think of some learning experience outside of school. For this activity an "external" learning activity, or one outside of school, is fine. The task is to discover what elements of the experience made it interesting and compelling. The goal is to incorporate those elements into schoolwork as often as possible.

Opportunities:

This activity is an opportunity to refocus and redefine your child's opinions about learning. Encourage your child to understand that learning can be fun and engaging.

Thinking about learning is an aspect of what educators call *meta-cognition*, or thinking about thinking. It involves reflecting on a past learning experience that contained the elements of success and determining what those elements are. This is one of the most powerful skills your child can have for understanding how to learn.

By the time you have finished this activity, you will have talked with your child about effort and ability, the three parts of learning, your child's particular style of learning, and the purpose of homework. You will also have discussed his or her experiences of powerful learning.

Chapter 5

HOMEWORK AND LEARNING STYLES

"In high school my daughter could study only while walking up and down the stairs in our house. She said it worked even better in college, where her dorm had five flights of stairs."

— A Midwest Mother

The Kaleidoscope Profile®

Understanding Learning Styles Differences

Homework can be a source of conflict between parents and children. Often such conflict arises due to confusion between parents and children who don't share the same learning styles.

Many conflicts that arise at home are due to simple style differences. For example, a fifth grader named Cory has a strong auditory preference. Whenever his family considered going to a movie, Cory got the newspaper and read all the possible choices out loud, including reviews and plot descriptions for all of them. The rest of his family found his reading difficult to follow and was often annoyed listening to him, since they could choose a movie based on much less information about it. Cory in turn became frustrated when no one wanted to listen or seemed to care.

The effort his family has made to realize their learning differences helps them understand one another's behaviors and needs without making judgments.

The family members have all learned to give a little so everyone feels more comfortable. Cory still reads about movies, and there is a set time when he only reads about those movies the family might want to see. Then they sit and discuss the movie selection. They have all developed better listening skills and the movie selection has become an enjoyable family ritual. Cory feels more comfortable and included, and rest of the family knows that any commitment to this auditory activity has a planned limit.

Mutual respect, teamwork, and meeting one another's needs can be a beneficial result of knowing one another's learning style.

Finding the Appropriate Homework Setting

For years the traditional homework setting included a well-lighted desk in a quiet part of the house where distractions were minimal. This was supposed to be the "right" atmosphere for doing homework. In other words, to succeed in homework, children had to be alone, without any conversation, music, or television. Children were expected to sit for an hour or more working through all their homework.

This traditional style of doing homework is actually most effective for visual students. The visual preference, however, represents less than half the student population. Other students may find such an environment very ineffective. They may need to do homework in the living room with the television on.

Finding the Appropriate Homework Style

Settings and styles for doing homework can influence how well or if homework is done. Jonathan wouldn't do his homework unless he was standing at the kitchen counter. His mother insisted that he do his homework in his room at his desk, but under those circumstances it didn't get done. Finally she realized she had a choice: have her son do his homework, or have him sit at his desk. She chose for him to do his homework.

Jonathan was a kinesthetic learner in first grade in a very academic school, and he was doing an hour of homework per night, which is far too much for a seven-year-old. Not surprisingly, every night there was an unpleasant two- or three-hour struggle to get him to finish his one hour of homework.

The mother decided to experiment with different methods of getting Jonathan to do his homework. She knew that kinesthetic students are active, needing to move around a great deal and wanting to be engaged in many activities at once. She decided to let Jonathan pick his own times to do the work and also let him decide how long he would work at a stretch. The only rules were that his homework had to be done right and that it had to be finished by a given deadline. Doubtful, she told Jonathan after school one day that he could do his homework whenever he chose, but that it must be finished by the time he went to school in the morning. He agreed. His homework that evening involved using a board with twelve quadrants to categorize fifty small objects according to set rules.

His mother was tempted to reprimand Jonathan when he rushed off to play with his brother rather than starting on the assignment. But she held off, and to her surprise she found him working on the assignment the next time she looked, about twenty minutes later. He worked for about ten minutes, then left. When he came back, he informed her that he was working again and told her what he had accomplished. This off-and-on process went on all evening. When he went to bed with only three quarters of his homework done, he said, "Don't worry, Mom. I'll complete it tomorrow." Knowing the child's typical foot-dragging in the morning, she doubted he would finish, but she decided to carry on with the experiment and simply nodded.

When she got up in the morning, Jonathan was finishing up the assignment. He had risen early to work on it, had left again, then gone back to finish up after breakfast. He was ready to go to school on time with a completed assignment.

His mother was amazed that Jonathan had been self-directed, had finished the work, and had done well with such an off-and-on process. Since she was a visual learner, her son's kinesthetic style differed greatly from how she would have done the assignment. Now that she has learned to be comfortable with his ways of getting assignments done, homework is a much easier and happier experience for both of them. Jonathan doesn't always get his homework done, but he's much more consistent and self-directed than he used to be.

Jonathan's mother recognized that her son had a learning style that was quite different from hers, and she allowed him the freedom to explore his own best ways of working.

The ultimate goal of allowing your child to determine what homework settings and styles work best is to free him or her to engage fully in the subject and purpose of the homework. Doing so will help your child become an enthusiastic and successful learner.

Summary:

- Understanding each other's different learning and working styles can help you and your child achieve success in any project you undertake together.

Activity 9: Homework Experiments

Time: Variable

Goals:

1. Help your child learn to sense which conditions "feel" right for his or her own best learning experience.

2. Notice the environment your child prefers to work in.

3. Improve the effort your child puts into homework.

Activity:

This activity has four elements for homework experimentation: time, place, physical settings, and emotional questions. Under your supervision, have your child experiment with several of these elements, or simply discuss them. Keep track of the elements that make homework more pleasant, even if they are minor improvements.

Experiment about once a week, with each element separately and then combine them until you find the optimal setting for your child. Experiment by introducing new settings to settings that work for your child. For instance, if you find that your child likes to do his or her homework right after school, encourage your child to do his or her homework right after school in the kitchen, then in the living room, until you find the best place to do homework matches the best time.

Some of the following experiments will appeal to one particular learning style more than others. When applicable, the experiments have been identified according to which learning style(s) they are most likely to benefit, using (K) for kinesthetic, (T) for tactual, (A) for auditory, and (V) for visual.

Time Experiments:
Ask your child **when** he or she would like to do homework:

- After school. • After dinner. • All at one time. (V & A)

- In the morning before school (if possible).

- A little at a time (spread from after school to the next morning before school). (K)

Whatever response your child gives, try the experiment below. Two measures of success are:

1. How your child feels.
   (More comfortable? Was it easier to work?)

2. Whether the homework is done well. (Is it complete? Neat? Correct?)

Have your child do his or her homework at three of the five times listed above. Experiment more than once to find out what times are consistently better.

Place Experiments:
Experiment with **where** your child studies:

- His or her room. (T & V)
- Kitchen. (A & K)
- Living room. (A, K, & T)
- Family room. (A & T)
- Brother or sister's room. (A & T)
- Porch. (K & T)
- Library. (V & T)
- Alone. (V & T)
- With other family members nearby. (T)
- With all children in the home doing homework together. (A & T)
- Other.

You decide which of these places are appropriate, but give your child at least three options. On a piece of paper, list what characteristics your child identifies as being the most helpful for him or her to do homework.

Physical Setting Experiments:

Determine **where** your child does his or her homework. Since there can be a great variation in how work is done, this experiment has far more possibilities. Try several experiments, always remembering there is no "right" way as long as the work is done well.

Sitting at a:
- Desk. (V)   • Table.   • Low coffee table. (T)

Position:
- Standing at a kitchen counter. (V & T)

- Lying on a bed or couch. (V & T)

- Lying on the floor. (V & T)

- Walking. (K & T)

- Sitting in a chair with no table or desk. (T & V)

- Other (beanbag chair, leaning back on chair while sitting on the floor, etc.). (K & T)

Lighting:
- Low lights. (T & A)

- Bright lights. (K & V)

- A single desk lamp. (V)

- Yellow (V), white, fluorescent lighting, or natural sunlight.

Activity:
- Walking while studying. (K)

- Rocking while studying. (K)

- Using a hand exerciser while studying. (T & K)

- Listening to music while studying. (If you experiment with music, start by playing music that has no words, such as slow classical music, before listening to faster, more modern music with words.) (A & T)

- Studying with friends or classmates. (A & T)

- Having snacks and drinks available while studying.

- Having a soft blanket around shoulders. (T)

Emotional Questions:

Have a conversation with your child about how he or she **feels** emotionally about doing homework. As the parent, you influence the emotional mood of the homework experience.

How does your child feel about homework?

- Always a chore.

- Sometimes enjoyable or interesting.

- Always something to look forward to.

- Usually enjoys the challenges and getting it done.

- Other.

Once your child has identified how he or she feels about homework, find out why. The questions below can act as an emotional barometer for the issue of homework in the family environment.

- What importance is homework given in the family? (What reasons for doing it does the family offer?)

- Do the family's feelings about homework make it more difficult or unpleasant?

- Does your child feel encouraged to do it?

- What kind of help can he or she expect? (What are your ideas about helping with homework, and how do you communicate those ideas?)

- Do other family activities interfere with your child's opportunity to do homework?

- What are your child's feelings about his or her ability to do the homework (for example, pessimistic, embarrassed, confident, challenged, bored, frustrated)?

There are no suggestions for what you should do or not do about the family's attitudes toward homework or what the correct place is for homework in family life. It's important that you know where there are conflicts concerning homework, if there are any. Once you have some answers to the emotional questions, you're in a better position to deal with any issues that might have been uncovered. The emotional feeling of the homework process in the family is an important one for your child, regardless of learning preference.

Challenges:

This activity asks your child to try different ways of doing homework. Note that a child who is not naturally experimental may resist this. A child with a strong sense of "right and wrong" regarding how homework "should" be done may also find the activities awkward. You might need to avoid asking too many questions until your child has done a number of the experiments. Then you can ask which one your child liked or which one seemed to produce the best work.

Because experimenting with these elements is an involved activity completed over several evenings, planning and follow-through may be necessary to help your child experiment. Don't try more than one or two experiments in an evening. More would be too many. It's also important to go over the experiment with your child afterwards, asking questions such as "How did it feel?" and "How did it work?"

Opportunities:

The greatest opportunity these homework experiments offer is giving your child a sense that he or she can find a better and more efficient way of doing homework. Having found that way, your child can become an active, lifelong learner. Be open to your child's own experimentation. Try out his or her ideas, even if it's obvious to you the ideas won't work. You may also find yourself thinking of additional ways not mentioned here to improve the homework experience. Try them, too, if your child is interested.

By working through the activities and discussions, you have laid a strong foundation for the activities and learning experiments that make up the second half of this book.

PART II

Learning Styles and the Three Parts of Learning

Now that you understand the basics of learning styles and where your child fits in, you are ready to learn more about the three types of learning strategies: retention, understanding, and application. To review:

- **Retention** is memorizing information and skills and being able to recall them when necessary.

- **Understanding** is the ability to see connections and relationships among the different aspects of what has been learned.

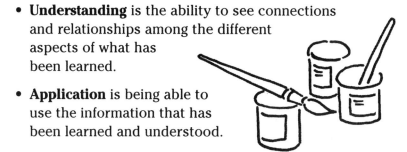

- **Application** is being able to use the information that has been learned and understood.

Below is an overview of the connections between learning styles and these three parts of learning.

Kinesthetic: Desires physical actions with physical things.

- **Retention:** Memorizes by linking words with actions, such as hand movements or dance. Uses physical objects like lettered blocks to memorize words starting with the letters on the blocks.

- **Understanding:** Represents the information physically, as in putting cards with words on them together to make sentences, or acting out the meanings of spelling words.

- **Application:** Uses what is learned. Relates most readily to projects, real-life activities, simulations, and other concrete/hands-on uses of knowledge and skills. For instance, finds adding and subtracting in a check register more interesting than doing 20 problems on a worksheet.

Tactual: Desires relationships, feelings, and interactions with people and things.

- **Retention:** Works well comparing and contrasting information about different but related subjects (such as mammals and amphibians). Enjoys telling how he or she feels about a character in a story.

- **Understanding:** Wants to play creatively with relations and feelings. Looks at information in different ways.

- **Application:** Enjoys projects, activities and real-life situations as kinesthetic learners do. Is more engaged if people, self-expression, and personal growth are also involved.

Auditory: Enjoys hearing, discussing, speaking out loud.

- **Retention:** Likes songs, chants, and rhymes, such as "*i* before *e* except after *c*" or singing the Presidents' names. Enhances memory by hearing and discussing what is to be memorized. Finds tape recording notes and playing them back very effective.

- **Understanding:** Likes to talk about issues in an open discussion that can lead to new insights. Uses debates, teaching others, explaining lessons, and quizzing others in study groups to increase understanding.

- **Application:** Learning applications that appeal to auditory learners involve group work, discussion, and opportunities to verbally explore the ways in which to apply knowledge.

Visual: Enjoys seeing, examining, and considering.

- **Retention:** Learns best by creating flash cards, pictures, and symbols linked to memorization. Many of the typical memorization tactics use visual aids.

- **Understanding**: Uses various reading materials with complementary/opposing viewpoints, pictures, and details. Wants many details to consider quietly.

- **Application:** Benefits from opportunities to create visual applications of information, as in displays, dioramas, pictures, and collages.

The following chapters address how to apply the three types of learning (retention, understanding, and application) to the different learning styles (kinesthetic, tactual, visual, and auditory) in order to optimize your child's homework experiences.

Chapter 6

HOMEWORK STRATEGIES FOR RETENTION

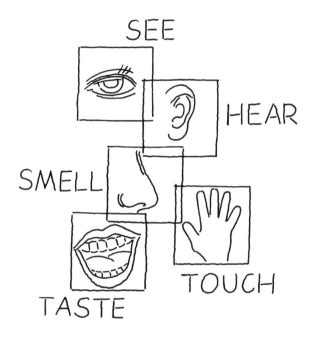

"We usually recall a piece of learning by remembering the context of emotions, sounds, smells, and locations associated with it. . . . This means that when we recall the circumstances (context) in which the learning took place, we also can recall the content of that learning."

— Terence Parry, Author

The Kaleidoscope Profile®

This chapter of *Homework and Kids: A Parent's Guide* offers retention strategies to help your child memorize important information, concepts, and skills. Some strategies can be used with any subject, while others are subject-specific.

Learning preferences also apply to memory. Physical memory strategies, such as associating hand gestures with words or feelings, help kinesthetic and tactual learners to remember, while visual learners remember what they see more readily. Chants, songs, and verbal word plays appeal to auditory learners wanting to memorize information.

Four methods that help the brain remember are **chunking**, **hooks**, **association**, and **repetition**. These methods are basic to any effort to memorize.

Chunking is taking several similar pieces of information and grouping them, or breaking up a large amount of information into smaller, more manageable groups. Four to seven pieces of information are the norm, which is why phone numbers and credit card accounts are chunked into three- and four-number groups (such as 800-555-1212).

Hooks help set information into memory through the use of music, rhymes, and word plays. Examples include "*i* before *e* except after *c*"; or the "Presidents Song," in which students sing the names of all the U.S. Presidents; or the use of hand gestures for the steps in division. Visual symbols and pictures can also work.

Association is linking something new to something that is already known. If the word *cat* is already memorized, for example, saying *kitten* is like *cat* will help a child remember *kitten* as well. Associating facts to be memorized with memorable or pleasant experiences also works as a memory association.

Repetition means repeating the information to be memorized several times — at least three times usually. The repetition doesn't have to be done the same way every time to be effective; for example, speaking, writing, and acting out a spelling word is repetition.

Use any strategies below that appeal to you and your child because any can prove to be effective for helping your child — they all support memorization. (You will also find a number of activities suitable for each learning style in Performance Learning Systems' online parenting course "Homework and Study Strategies.")

Kinesthetic Activities

For kinesthetic learners, large body movements and activities are important aids to memory. These students memorize best by moving around and "experiencing" information physically.

✗ Big Words

Have your child write what is to be memorized in the air. Or, your child can write on a large pad of paper, a chalkboard, or on the sidewalk with chalk — the bigger the arm movements, the better.

✗ Flash Cards

- Using flash cards is a useful technique, but have your child perform an action with them such as throwing them into a hat as they are memorized.

- Make the flash cards colorful and large, and have your child stand and drop each card as he or she finishes with it.

- Try to include a variety of movements. For instance, your child can sit and then jump up when answering questions on the cards.

✗ Memory Game

Make memorization into a game. Use at least 16 3" x 5" cards and write questions on half of them. Write the answers to the questions on the other half.

Turn all the cards face down in equal rows. Players take turns turning over two cards to find a match between a question and an answer. If the cards don't match, the player then turns them down again and the next player takes a turn. If the two cards match, the player keeps the cards and keeps on playing until failing to make a match.

The player with the most cards at the end of the game is the winner.

✕ Math Steps

Using chalk, draw math problems on the garage floor or sidewalk, making the numbers quite large.

Then have your child "walk" through the math process. For instance, "carrying 2" would require stepping up to the appropriate place on the drawn problem and writing the "2" in.

Tactual Activities

For the tactual learner, the personal touch enhances memory. Small movements, comfort, and individual expression are important tools for memorizing.

✕ Memory Places

Have your child designate a place (such as a bed or couch) and a position (such as lying down or sitting) as her or his "memory place." While it can also be used for study, the primary function of this location is to aid in memorization.

Creating a memory place uses association to aid retention.

✕ The Interview

Have your child write down questions about the information to be memorized then interview other family members and friends to see if they know the answers. Encourage your child to help them by giving hints about the information.

✕ Puzzle It

Write down important facts to be memorized on a colored piece of card stock or construction paper. Then decorate the paper by coloring on it and drawing some pictures. Cover the paper with clear contact paper if you want. Then cut the paper into at least 16 irregularly shaped pieces to look like a jigsaw puzzle, and give them to your child to put together.

The task enhances memorizing in two ways: it requires small motor movements, while also requiring your child to use written facts to help figure out how to work the puzzle.

✘ First Impression

Have your child write down the information to be memorized on slips of paper and put them in a bag. Then have your child pull out a slip of paper and explain how she or he feels about the information. Does your child like the words? Do the words bring up memories? This can become a dramatic activity if your child acts out the feelings or impressions.

This activity is especially helpful for math and science words, as they are abstract and often more difficult to learn.

The child continues to choose slips of paper and says what impressions each word incites.

Auditory Activities

Auditory learners remember what they hear and what they say. Any activity that encourages them to listen and talk enhances memory.

✘ Memory Discussions

Have your child's friends over to study. Give them a term or fact to be memorized, and ask them to discuss it, relating whatever they remember about it. When one fact has been discussed to a stopping point, give them another term or fact.

This technique can be a game to see how much information the group can come up with concerning a particular term or fact.

✘ Copying Terms

Have your child copy terms, words, or formulas to be memorized. Your child says the terms first, then writes them down, then reads them aloud. This activity is particularly effective for spelling tests.

✘ Tag Team Memory

Have one child begin by reading or reciting the beginning of a list of items to be memorized. For example, a child could spell out the first three spelling words on a list or state the first three parts of a times table.

The child then says "tag" to another child, who continues where the first child left off. Each child must read or recite for ten seconds, which you can indicate by holding up fingers or tapping a pen. When ten seconds is up, the child speaking can "tag" someone else, who then continues for another ten seconds. It's fun to see how fast everyone can speak and go through the tag.

✗ Musical Flash Cards

Group the items to be memorized in a logical manner such as the nine times table, the East Coast states, or the first five spelling words on a list. Then choose some wordless music on an audiotape or CD your child likes. Have your child recite the information to be memorized as the music plays. Continue playing the music until all items are memorized.

You can use this process for as many as six groups of items to be memorized (but no more than six). Play different music for each group while memorizing.

After a break, play the music and see if your child can remember the facts that go with it. Run through this once or twice. When your child hears or thinks of the music later, the memorized items will be easier to recall.

Visual Activities

Visual learners remember what they see. Providing visual cues such as diagrams, notes, demonstrations, and pictures, help the visual learner memorize and recall information.

✗ Symbols and Pictures

Have your child draw pictures or symbols for items on cards (for instance, a top hat for Abraham Lincoln or a pie chart for fractions). When the card is shown, have your child recall all he or she can remember about what the picture represents.

✖ Play Pictionary

Play with your family or friends, or with your child alone, taking turns drawing. The game is played like the commercial game of the same name.

Each player or one player on a team takes a turn picking a card and drawing a picture to represent the term written on the card. If only you and your child are playing, each of you tries to guess what term the other's drawing represents. If you are playing with teams, one team member draws and the others try to guess what term the drawing represents. You can also time how long each player or team takes to come up with the correct term. Whoever takes the shortest time wins.

✖ Mind Mapping from Memory

Have your child take a large piece of paper and in the middle write the title of a main topic to be memorized, such as "Products Produced by a Country" or "Parts of the Respiratory System." Then have your child draw a circle around the title with lines radiating out from the circle. At the end of each line your child will write one fact or point about the main topic. Have your child write down all the points he or she can remember. Then ask your child to check to see if he or she missed any points.

Use different colors for different components. This mind map can be posted in your child's room as a visual aid.

✖ Matching and Grouping

Using several 3" x 5" cards, have your child write down one "step" of a concept, process, or event per card. Math rules, science processes, or parts of a particular historical event work particularly well for this activity. Your child will need to think of at least three steps per process. Then mix up the cards, and ask your child to group them in the right order.

Once you and your child start experimenting with these memory activities, you will observe several outcomes:

1. You will see that some activities work better for your child than others.

2. You and your child will modify the activities to produce better results.

3. You both will think of other kinds of activities to aid your child's memory.

4. You will remember different memorizing tricks you yourself learned in school.

Most importantly, remember that this is a learning process in itself, and that you and your child will get better at it as you practice experimenting with the memory strategies.

Summary:

- There are four memory strategies that help your child's brain to remember information: chunking, hooks, association, and repetition. This chapter presented a number of activities applying these methods and others to the four sensory learning styles.

Chapter 7

HOMEWORK STRATEGIES FOR UNDERSTANDING

"What I hear, I forget.
What I see, I remember.
What I do, I understand."

— Old Chinese Proverb

The Kaleidoscope Profile®

The part of learning we call "understanding" is extremely important, but it rarely gets the attention it deserves. This lack of attention is because understanding:

- Takes far more time to accomplish than either retention or application.

- Cannot be measured accurately.

- Is difficult to plan for.

- Has an infinite number of qualities and layers, unlike retention and application, which are more concrete.

Many times the failure to memorize or apply information and skills successfully is due to a lack of understanding. We have all had the frustrating experience of not understanding something until we received just the right explanation or had the right experience.

> *Most often we acquire solid understanding*
> *when we have multiple experiences*
> *of the same information.*

The following activities provide a wide variety of ways you and your child can experience concepts, skills, and facts that need to be understood and learned.

As in the previous chapter, these activities are grouped by learning style because matching your child's style to the activities increases the odds that a particular activity will work for him or her. However, there is a great deal of crossover among these activities; for example, many kinesthetic activities can work well for an auditory child. Experiment and use the ones that work for you and your child.

The process of understanding is very much like child's play. The point of play is to increase children's understanding of the world around them. Children act out situations and relationships with different variations over and over. They "play" with information by varying it often with no effort to solve anything or "get it right," but rather to get a sense of it and gain a better understanding. The activities in this chapter support that kind of experience.

For example, the teacher in one school's math department found word problems difficult for most students to solve. One such problem asked students to determine the height of a tree by knowing the length of its shadow as well as the height and shadow length of a man nearby. Instead of trying to solve the problem, the teacher asked her students to make models and representations of the problem using any approach they wished. Some very clever models were made. One student created real shadows using a desk lamp.

Even though these students had poor math skills and had been unable to do many word problems in the past, more than half of them figured out the answer to the problem as part of their model making process — and they did the calculations in their heads! One student was amazed she found the answer, because she was terrified of math and hadn't even been trying to solve the problem, only make a paper model of it.

The following strategies look at the concepts, facts, or methods to be understood in new and different ways that engage as many senses as possible. Generally, these strategies provide experiences of the information to be learned rather than the "right" answers. Note that even though these strategies are limited to the subjects of math and English, most of them are general enough that you can expand and apply them to other subjects your child studies in school. (There is also a broad range of similar activities in Performance Learning Systems' online parenting course "Homework and Study Strategies.")

Kinesthetic Activities

Kinesthetic strategies take a problem and make it physical, as in the Spelling Twister activity. Often these strategies require using physical objects. You may be able to borrow some objects from school, but items you find around the house can work just as well.

✘ Math (Physical Representations)

Any effort to memorize math facts and skills can be aided by physical representations of numbers, words, concepts, and even basic skills themselves. Your child can do many activities with such representations; for example, grouping them together by similarities or making drawings of mathematical processes sufficiently large enough to walk through.

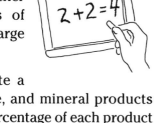

For instance, your child may create a pie graph by finding animal, vegetable, and mineral products in your house and determining what percentage of each product is represented. Your child can graph these percentages as he or she determines what they are.

✘ Math (Measuring the Family)

Measuring can be an enjoyable activity for the whole family. You can lay family members down on large sheets of paper and trace around them as well as measure them. This activity provides practice with math processes as well as units of measurements (feet, inches, yards, and centimeters).

Using the measurements of each family member, you can ask questions such as: "How many little brothers laid end to end would it take to make a mile?", "If you added the lengths of every family member's right arm, how long would that be?", "If everyone stood on someone else's head, how high would the family reach?"

✘ English (Spelling Twister)

Write spelling words on 3" x 5" cards (one to a card), and lay the cards out on the floor. Choose a word and call it out, placing one of your hands or feet on the card.

Variation: Lay out cards with only half a word on each. Players have to put their right hand on the first part of the word called out and their left foot on the second part. Then they must call out another word and put their left hand and right foot on its parts. This presents a new kind of "word recognition."

✗ English (Building a Paragraph/Essay)

If your child has to write a paragraph, have him or her write individual sentences about facts and information in the paragraph on separate strips of paper.

Then ask your child to move the sentences to build the paragraph. While a child can do this using "cut and paste" on a computer, physically moving the sentences on a flat surface is a different experience altogether and is therefore valuable for understanding.

You can also use this activity to build essays (at least four paragraphs).

Tactual Activities

Tactual children desire harmonious, comfortable experiences and craft-like activities. Like kinesthetic children, tactual learners benefit from having physical objects to manipulate.

✗ Math (Triple Tape)

When your child is learning a math process, record three separate explanations to be replayed. The recording could include your child's teacher or you yourself explaining how to do the math, your child reading an explanation from the math book, and another family member or friend paraphrasing the book. The explanations do not have to be long, but they should use different examples and wording.

When your child listens to the tape, he or she has three different experiences of the same information.

✕ Math (Group Discussion)

This activity works best when several classmates or family members participate. A math problem is shown or described, then each member of the group says how he or she thinks the problem can be solved and what the answer is. There is no time limit — everyone may take as long as they like. A general discussion starts after each person has had a turn to answer.

Variation 1. Have one person give his or her idea for solving a problem, then have the others ask questions or give corrections. Have enough problems so that each person gets a turn to solve one.

Variation 2. The entire group discusses each problem together.

Variation 3. Each member of the group offers part of the solution to a problem. Someone with a timer can give the signal to stop and move on to the next person. Each person has five to ten seconds to give as much information as he or she can. If someone gets stuck, the problem is thrown open to group discussion.

✕ English (Spelling Stories)

When you sit down with your child to read or tell a story, have the child's spelling list with you. If you're making the story up, include the spelling words as you go along. If you're reading, be creative: improvise your reading so that you're able to work in the spelling words. Ask your child to give you a sign whenever he or she hears one of the words. For tactual learners, understanding often comes in story form.

✕ English (Writing Exercise)

A tactual child often enjoys cursive writing, calligraphy, and graphic arts. Have your child use different forms of writing to distinguish between different parts of a sentence, essay, or story. For example, the forms may vary between cursive and printing, or your child may use different styles of calligraphy or even more ornate forms of writing — even designs and illustrations. (You might want to clear this with the teacher for any assignments your child must turn in.)

A variation is to have your child use different colors — pens, pencils, markers, crayons — to make distinctions.

Auditory Activities

Auditory learners talk and listen their way to understanding. Activities usually need to include talking to others as well as receiving and giving verbal explanations.

✗ Math (Explain and Do)
Have your child explain verbally what he or she is doing in each step when solving a problem. If there is confusion or a lack of understanding, the place in the process where he or she is struggling becomes evident. It is important to have your child write the step as he or she explains it.

✗ Math (Twenty Questions)
Think of a math procedure or term your child has to learn. Your child has twenty "yes" or "no" questions she or he can ask to figure out what term you're thinking of. This game should use a limited list of possible terms (say ten to twenty). Let your child look at the list while asking questions. Start with easy terms and short lists first.

✗ English (Story Tapes)
If your child is assigned writing sentences for spelling words or a writing story, have him or her first repeat the sentences or the story out loud into a tape recorder. Then your child can write while listening to the tape. Often an auditory learner can jump-start the writing process this way.

✗ English (Reading with Expression)
Have your child give a dramatic reading of a story, report, or sentences that he or she has written. Correct spelling and necessary punctuation often become apparent when a child reads with inflection and intonation. This can be fun and challenging when the sentences are rather dry and technical.

A variation is that you read your child's writing with dramatic flair and even have your child "coach" you on how to do it.

Visual Activities

Visual learners often take the longest to consider learning and provide the least feedback for parents on any learning activities. Seeing is understanding for the visual learner.

✗ Math (Diagram It)

Have your child diagram a math procedure with numbered steps and examples; for example, your child may place the steps in a chart. These charts are called graphic organizers and can be of great help to visual learners intent on understanding concepts, processes, and relationships.

✗ Math (Hunting Mistakes)

This activity has three variations. In the first you do a math problem that your child has learned as he or she watches. At some point you will purposely make a mistake, and your child should catch the mistake.

The second variation is that you write out all the steps of a problem, making one mistake. Your child then reviews the steps to find the mistake.

The third variation is that your child writes out the problem, purposely making a mistake, and then friends or family members find it. Like drawing a picture upside down to get a deeper sense of drawing, purposely making mistakes gives another "sense" of the math process.

✗ English (Story and Sentence Starters)

If your child is having difficulty getting started on a story or a series of sentences, find pictures in magazines. The pictures may suggest details that your child can use to begin the story or sentences. While reading and writing are visual mediums, giving your visual learner concrete pictures can help jump-start the writing process.

✗ English (Right and Wrong)

Use three 3" x 5" cards for each spelling word. On two, spell the word incorrectly, and on the third spell it correctly. Mark the back of the card that has the correctly-spelled word. Then show all three cards to your child, and have your child try to pick the correctly spelled word.

A more challenging method is to write your child's spelling words on 3" x 5" cards, but spell some of them incorrectly. Use the cards like flash cards. Your child decides if a word is spelled correctly or incorrectly.

Make two card piles, one for words your child identifies as correctly spelled and the other for words identified as incorrectly spelled. After going through all of the cards, check the two piles to determine which were correctly identified.

Summary:

- Understanding is a central part of learning.

- In order to fully understand an assignment, your child may need to be exposed to it multiple times and in varying ways.

Chapter 8

HOMEWORK STRATEGIES FOR APPLICATION

"Teaching for knowledge cannot be separated from teaching for meaning — or helping students understand the purpose of what they are asked to do in the classroom."

— Dale Parnell, Author

The Kaleidoscope Profile®

Application uses information students have practiced, remembered, and understood.

You can increase your child's learning success by identifying the reasons he or she has for learning a particular fact or skill and the ways it can be used.

There are three ways you can help your child apply his or her learning.

1. Real-Life Applications
Your child can use what he or she learns from homework at home or any other place outside of school.

2. Feeding Your Child's Passions
From time to time your child will become especially interested in particular topics, such as dinosaurs or space exploration. Showing your child how to use reading, math, or science learning with these "passions" can increase your child's ability to apply knowledge in these subjects.

3. School Assignments and Tests
Work with your child or the teachers to encourage your child's success with assignments and tests.

Real-Life Applications

The following learning applications relate to family activities and should be treated as informal efforts. As a parent, you can give small tasks and responsibilities to your child that use different skills he or she is learning, especially in reading, language arts, and math.

For example, your child can help you shop, buy, and put away groceries while applying what he or she has learned. Start small and slowly increase the number and complexity of the tasks you ask your child to do.

When you are shopping, have your child read aisle signs, food labels, prices, and food ingredients. The seemingly simple task of finding a can of corn from among all the canned vegetables in a supermarket can be a real test of reading ability and picture recognition. You can ask a fourth- or fifth-grade child to get the twelve-ounce size or the lowest priced item. Asking your son or daughter to tell you whether a prepared food contains mushrooms is a test of several reading skills. When your child learns new skills, provide opportunities for testing them with you.

Your child can use math skills by adding up grocery prices or doing some comparison shopping. Start with a short list of grocery purchases before asking your child to add up longer lists. Even having your child record prices as you put items in your basket can strengthen writing and math skills. Also, most grocery stores have a clock. Asking your child to check the time or to figure out how much time you spent at the grocery store is a great application of time concepts learned in school.

The day-to-day activities of keeping a home can be an adventure in math, reading, writing, and telling time. Cooking requires following written directions, estimating time, and planning. The same is true of housekeeping chores, especially if the tasks have to be divided evenly among other brothers and sisters. In all of these chores, you don't have to create a formal activity or assignment — just ask questions that are already part of the cooking or chores.

Continually draw attention to how school learning can be used at home. Your encouragement plus the delegation of small tasks will strengthen the learning experience of application.

Your child can also help plan a family outing or vacation. Even with a simple picnic, he or she can estimate costs (including gas), figure time requirements, and work out a division of family responsibilities such as who will pack the food.

Any work around the house — repairs, washing the car, and most general upkeep — requires the use of tools. Using tools often involves measuring, using particular sizes, and buying materials. All of these skills require math, reading, and measuring skills.

The best way to approach these application activities and challenges with your child is to go for the "sure win." Ask your child to do things you are confident he or she can do well and easily, then increase the challenges based on first successes.

Be alert to everyday circumstances and your child's natural desire to be part of the adult action. Sometimes the best learning experiences happen with just a little nudge rather than as the result of detailed plans.

Feeding Your Child's Passions

Feeding your child's passions offers opportunities for him or her to exercise skills and knowledge. The only potential drawback is that you can't plan what will interest your child. You have to be responsive to opportunities as they come up.

For example, one father had a wonderful time discussing the solar system with his fourth-grade daughter when she became fascinated with the subject. The two of them did projects together that weren't even school assignments — his daughter just wanted to do them.

At one point she laid out a long roll of butcher paper and attempted to plot the distances of the various planets from the sun. She wanted to make her picture "to scale" but didn't know how to do that. The task required a great deal of math, from equivalents to measuring distance and determining what scale would fit the butcher paper. The father encouraged his daughter on the project while she practiced her math skills. In this situation, a passion about the solar system led to a passion about math. Encourage your child's passions and he or she may have a similar experience.

School Assignments and Tests

Your child will take many types of tests and complete a variety of assignments during his or her school career. Some tests and assignments will be easier to do than others, often according to how they suit your child's learning style. There are ways to support your child, regardless of the assignment and your child's learning style.

For example, one child might be a whiz at multiple-choice tests but continually fail on essay tests. As a parent, you can work with his or her teacher[s] to ensure that your child learns effectively and that school is as meaningful as possible. You want your child to have choices for "proving" what he or she has learned. This "proof of learning" can be a test, but the test can be oral as well as written; or the proof of learning can be achieved through written work, oral discourse, or even through a project.

Here are some methods for working with the teacher as you support your child:

Meet with your child's teacher[s]. At the beginning of the year before any issues develop, meet with your child's teacher and discuss how the teacher tests and grades. Hopefully there will be a variety of assessment methods. Then ask if the teacher will consider alternative assignments and tests that fit your child's learning style, and find out what types he or she would consider. Most teachers will acknowledge that any particular test does not serve all children equally well.

Work with your child. Sooner or later you will find that your child has a frustrating project or test. The problems will almost always lie in your child's disliking the type of project or test rather than the subject itself. For example, in teaching the U.S. Constitution, a teacher may assign students the task of writing it out in its entirety and then writing a report about it. Some students will find this easy, while for others it will be a huge challenge.

By taking the time to discuss your child's frustrations, you will be better equipped to help with any project.

How Much Help Should I Help?

This is a difficult question because there is no right answer. The goal is to help your child learn to complete his or her work independently or with only minimal assistance from you. The dilemma is that your child wants to answer a question or solve a problem, and you want to help, but you don't want to — and shouldn't — end up doing the work.

Here are some guidelines for determining how much to help your child and how much your child needs to work independently:

1. Take the time.
Helping your child complete assignments correctly is more important than supplying hasty or halfhearted assistance. You are a busy parent and it is quicker to give the answer than help the child find it. Unfortunately, this gets you and your child in the "quick fix" habit. Remember that you are the model for your child and that helping effectively once can eliminate the need to help several times later.

2. Have your child do the work.

When your child comes to you for help, ask questions about what the specific issues are rather than accepting the response, "I don't know how to do it." Clarifying the confusion trains your child to expect help rather than just an answer. Plus your child will put forth extra effort before coming to you if he or she knows you're not simply going to supply the answer.

3. Think about how your child might find an answer independently.

Consider ways your child can find the answer besides getting help from you. Help your child locate the appropriate source (e.g., dictionary or Internet) for the information in question. When your child comes to you with a similar question later, remind him or her to go to other resources first.

4. Keep in mind the learning process.

Consider the goals of a particular learning process: retention, understanding, or application. You and your child need to remember the following:

- Understand the task — What is your child being asked to learn or do?

- Organize, schedule, collect, and otherwise plan for large projects.

- Carry out the task (solve the problem or complete the assignment) and figure out whether or not it's correct.

- Determine if your child is presenting the work correctly. Presentation can include such things as your child's name written in the right-hand corner, neatness, or showing all work in a math problem.

As a parent, you want to give the time needed to help, and you don't want to make your child dependent on you. This challenge isn't met in one day, nor is it ever resolved once and for all. It's an ongoing task that you will learn to perform with increasing effectiveness as you work with your child.

Here are some ideas to use with your child:

- When your child becomes frustrated with a complicated problem, help by breaking the problem into parts. If your child can work through a problem step-by-step, it will seem less daunting and there can be many little "victories" along the way as steps are completed.

- It's quite natural for your child to want minimal help. Your child will let you know when your help is no longer needed by responding with some form of "Okay, I got it," or waving you away. Be sure to bow out as soon as you get the signal.

- Provide materials and a place to work. If your child needs something from the store or needs to use tools that can be used only in your presence, make an appointment with your child so he or she learns to make such requests ahead of time. This added responsibility teaches your child to plan ahead and be respectful of your time.

- Create a homework notebook with tabs for each subject. When your child asks you a question about a particular topic, he or she needs to write down the question and the answer on a sheet of paper and insert it in the notebook after the appropriate tab. The next time your child has a question, he or she must check whether the question has been answered before.

- If the difficulty is in doing or understanding a process such as writing or math, do one of the problems while your child watches. Work through a second problem while your child tells you what to do. Then do a problem where you tell your child what to do, and finally have your child do a problem while you watch.

- Give yourself a time limit for trying a technique. For instance, if you have been helping your child for five minutes and more help is needed, try another approach. If you have been helping with the same problem, question, or worksheet for ten minutes, your assistance isn't working. Encourage your child to try something else or go on to other work to give yourself and your child a break, then come back to the problem later.

- Designate what exactly you will or will not help with. For instance, you may help with review for a spelling test, but you won't tell your child how to spell a word (since he or she has a dictionary).

- You might want to create tokens called "help tokens." Limit the supply per help session. For example, give your child a homework question "quota," such as offering three to five "help tokens" per night. Once the tokens are used up, that's it. (An alternative for unused "help tokens" is to allow your child to accumulate them and cash them in for other options that take up your time, such as rides to the mall or to a friend's house.)

These ideas suggest ways to control and measure the time you spend helping your child. If your assistance is doing what it should, your child will be asking for less help throughout the school year. Helping your child effectively takes time, and the idea is to put yourself out of business as your child's homework guru.

Summary:

- Homework is an integral part of your child's "schoolwork." Continued success with homework demands a level of effective communication with your child's teachers.

- You are responsible for ensuring that your child's effort rather than your effort completes the task.

Chapter 9

LEARNING SUCCESS

"Genuine learning . . . is a process of discovery in which the student is the main agent, not the teacher."

— Mortimer J. Adler, Author

The Kaleidoscope Profile®

By now you have probably gained valuable insights about your child as a learner in terms of his or her own unique style. By completing the activities, you have probably had successful and unsuccessful experiments with your child. Keep using the successful methods as long as they work, and dismiss the others — or modify them so they do work for your child.

By using this book and tailoring the information to your child, you have been modeling the importance you place on his or her success in learning.

> ***Emphasizing your concern for your child's success is vital to his or her learning.***

Making Learning a Priority

If your child is going to be a successful learner, learning must be established in your family as an important goal. However, making learning a priority requires time, which can create conflicts within the family. Schoolwork can interfere with family plans. For example, some parents report that a major source of tension in the family is school and homework.

Your child may find that the demands of school and the demands of family are placing her or him in a difficult situation. One way to decrease potential conflict is to make some clear decisions about priorities regarding family planning, traditions, and daily procedures.

1. How important is schoolwork and school success?

While schoolwork does not need to be the most important thing in your child's life, you need to make a decision regarding how important it is to your family.

One family might sacrifice everything to see that schoolwork is done, planning around school schedules. Family activities are contemplated only when homework is finished. Another family will take the children out of school on a regular basis to go skiing or visit friends. The question is not which decision is "right," but whether each family is accomplishing its goals.

The first family sacrifices family time for school success. It should be no surprise that spending time with the family seems of secondary importance to their children. The second family should not be surprised if their children choose to play with friends instead of do their homework. In both cases, the priorities have been set by the family, and the children are adhering to them.

Your role as a parent is to decide how important schoolwork is to *your* family. Clear decisions about priorities help everyone in the family. For example, one approach is to say that school is your child's work. Just as your work consumes part of each day, so does your child's "job." While there may be times that you give up family activities due to "job" demands, you may decide that family has a higher priority than "work." Or you may decide that work takes higher priority. Each family must find their own answer, but determining priorities and adhering to them will benefit your family.

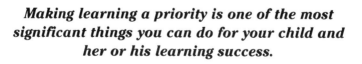

Making learning a priority is one of the most significant things you can do for your child and her or his learning success.

2. Does your family enjoy learning?

Some families like to discover new activities or hobbies and explore them together. A common family tradition is for everyone at the dinner table to tell one new thing learned that day. Another is for children to spend time telling parents what they learned at school or about their homework. Perhaps there are ongoing family activities that encourage learning that you could start doing with your children. Consider what kinds of activities the family can do to model continual learning or learning for the pure joy of it.

3. Do family members have learning goals?

Learning is always necessary for reaching new goals. You and your family can model this fact for your child by involving the whole family in learning situations.

For instance, a family might spend time learning about cars, the goal being the purchase of a family car. Children and parents could participate in the "research" and select whatever car is most suitable according to everyone's research.

Celebrating Learning Success

It's very important to celebrate your child's learning successes each day. A child who has exerted effort to successfully learn difficult concepts and skills deserves recognition for effort. Below are a few celebrations for you to try:

Rituals: Rituals are activities repeated on certain occasions to acknowledge important events until they become a firm part of a group's culture and history.

1. *Handshakes/Sayings*
   Use special handshakes or sayings when your child has completed homework or difficult assignments. Give "high" and "low" fives, or call out, "The homework master!" when he or she is done. Your child can also call out "All's clear!" and your family can respond with applause as a way to celebrate.

2. *A Ritual Response*

Try keeping a record of all the hours your child spends on homework. For example, one parent put a penny in a jar every evening for each half hour his child worked on homework. The pennies didn't add up to a lot of money at the end of the school year, but the sheer quantity of them gave the child a sense of accomplishing something impressive.

3. *Rewards*

Rewards can be simple things like serving dessert only after your child's homework is done. Or they can be a family outing or a reprieve from chores for a weekend. Maybe at the end of a week when your child has done all of his or her homework each day, you can take your child out to dinner or a movie.

4. *Wish lists*

When large homework projects have been assigned, ask your child what he or she wishes for when the project is done. It may be something big or small. But at the completion of the homework, some aspect of the wish should be fulfilled. For example, one ten-year-old boy wished for a big car. When he finished his homework project, his mother gave him a model of it.

5. *Celebrations and Parties*

Celebrations and parties don't have to be large or expensive. You can simply bring out party poppers and confetti. Or you can throw two-minute parties when important homework is finished or your child has received an especially good report card. Another idea is to play a funny song every time some particularly challenging school assignment has been finished.

Celebrations of effort are very important.
Use positive reinforcement to help your
child be a successful learner.

A Perspective on Learning

Learning is a natural process, which means that it doesn't develop in a linear fashion: A before B and B before C. It can be a fairly messy and lively activity. Many parents worry that if a child hasn't reached a particular level of learning by a certain year, all is lost. For example, some believe this is the case if a child can't read by the time he or she is in first grade. Learning doesn't use a formula or outline. Each child learns differently.

Learning is an ongoing process, and there are few absolutes for how it progresses or when.

Consider when your child learned to walk. The "normal" age range is somewhere between eight and 18 months. Yet if your child started walking at six months or at 20 months, your pediatrician probably wasn't concerned. No doctor "grades" your child on walking the way education often grades learning progress in subjects like reading. A pediatrician trusts the natural process. Your child will learn to walk when he or she is ready.

Trust that learning will take place when your child is ready.

Your child will learn what she or he needs to learn, especially if your child has your support and is allowed to progress at his or her own pace. The confidence you show in your child's ability to learn successfully gives him or her the confidence necessary to face difficulties in school and with homework.

Success in School

School as we know it was designed more than 100 years ago before people knew very much about learning. In the United States, educators unintentionally designed schoolwork to support certain learning style characteristics and not others. Traditional school organizations, therefore, don't meet certain learning needs — and neither do many alternative schools, for that matter.

Figure 7 describes what learning styles needs and strengths the traditional school addresses. While schools are changing their teaching methods, unmet learning needs are still an issue. If your child is having difficulty in school, perhaps the style of the school doesn't match your child's style. Having this knowledge can help you understand the situation so you can work with your child's teachers.

School Learning Matches and Mismatches

This chart is based on a generalization about traditional school systems in the United States at the time of publication. Individual schools can differ and often do. You may need to take the time to find out how your child's learning style matches or conflicts with the teaching practices in his or her school. This chart is also a generalization of learning style needs, which may be different for your child. The chart should help you find a place to start in understanding the relationship between school and your child.

Kinesthetic	**Learns best:** With a hands-on approach. With physical involvement in learning, projects, field trips, small group activities (two to three people). Through sports, science, computers, and P.E. When reading for action and "how to" rather than enjoyment. Studying for short periods or moving around while studying.	**Challenges in school:** Uncomfortable with typical school practices involving sitting still for longer periods, and remembering what is said versus what is done. Interpersonal skills challenge children who take an experimental approach to all issues.
Tactual	**Learns best:** Participating in activities and working with others. With graphics, writing, and social studies. Reading for pleasure and the feelings it invokes. Reading about people. Studying in own "personal space" at chosen times, often with family and friends.	**Challenges in school:** Traditional schools are not designed to meet individual needs. So this learner, who needs comfort, personal space, and opportunity for individual expression, is often uncomfortable and may not do well in school. Can have issues around being "too sensitive." If the student dislikes the teacher, it is harder for him or her to learn.

Figure 7: School Learning Matches and Mismatches

School Learning Matches and Mismatches		
Auditory	**Learns best:** Through classroom discussion, debate, group work, question and answer periods through phonics. Using self-expression as a form of thinking and learning. Enjoying music, drama, debate, and public speaking. Reading dialogue in books. Stopping to talk about a book. Talking to others from time to time while studying.	**Challenges in school:** Traditional schools expect students to be quiet and listen. Auditory students "talk too much" and gravitate toward social activities involving discussion. May be frustrated when everything is not open for discussion. Tend to be slower at studying and are distracted by sounds and conversations. Take verbal reprimands seriously.
Visual	**Learns best:** Reading and watching. Through quiet listening and testing. Doing English, math, art, and history. Reading, which is generally a joy for this student. Studying, as this student remembers what is seen. Can sit still for long periods.	**Challenges in school:** Traditional schools can match this student's style. Quiet and visually skilled, this student has little difficulty being an "average" student. Can fail to participate if no connections are made. Verbal self-expression can be difficult. Confidence produces a more expressive verbal student. Can want to be ignored in class and is easily overlooked by teachers in the rush of the day. Can internalize problems without resolving them or letting others know about them. Phonics is difficult for this student.

Figure 7: School Learning Matches and Mismatches

Learning styles are often overlooked in traditional school systems. In the chart above, you may have noticed traits your child exhibits, and some of those traits may contribute to your child's success or failure in school and learning. Knowing the issues your child faces prepares you to deal with them.

Summary:

- Learning must be an important family goal if your child is to be a successful learner.

- Celebrating your child's success is a powerful way to reinforce achievement and encourage future success.

- Learning is a natural, ongoing process that is different for each child. Trust the process.

- Your awareness of how traditional school approaches to learning affect your child can help your child succeed in school.

- Learning styles, statistics, and general school tendencies are not predictors of your child's success or lack of success. They represent information you can use to increase your child's learning success.

Activity 10: Setting Priorities
Time: 10 - 30 minutes

Goals:

1. Determine where learning and school fit into your family priorities.

2. Reinforce learning processes offered in this book that you want to use.

Activity:

Your answers to the questions below will provide a model your child follows in making decisions about school. Feel free to write down your answers on a separate piece of paper.

1. Where does schoolwork fall in the scheme of your daily life? Which family activities or concerns are important to you? Which are less important? For instance, your family probably believes that eating dinner is important. You would not forego a meal because of your child's homework, but you might forego watching television afterward if his or her homework wasn't completed.

   If friends invite your child over, do you insist that he or she finish all homework first, or do you allow your child to go? Do you sometimes compromise? What are the reasons behind your priorities?

2. What kinds of decisions can you expect your child to make about school and learning based on your conclusions above?

3. In the larger context, do you see your child going to college or doing something else after high school? Have you communicated your expectations to your child? How is school directly related to attending college or the other goals? If college attendance is a family expectation, the answers may seem obvious to you, but they may not be obvious to your child. Be clear in stating the benefits of college and the benefits of schoolwork as a precursor to college. If you find you're having a hard time describing that connection to your satisfaction, chances are good that your child will too. Whatever future you see for your child will be your child's first vision of the life he or she will consider, even if that vision later evolves into something else. You are therefore the one setting the first goals for your child's life. Be clear on what these goals are and how they relate to school and learning.

Remember: Learning is a critical set of life skills that makes all other skills possible.

4. Of the learning processes described below, select one or two that you would like to begin to reinforce in your family.

Remember: The amount of time you dedicate to the issue of learning directly influences the amount of time your child will dedicate to it.

Learning Time-Outs
Pick a time for a regular ten- to 15-minute discussion of what your child learns in school each day. This discussion may occur when your child comes home or just before bedtime. The actual time of the discussion isn't as important as the regularity of it.

A Common Family Time for Discussion of Learning

Pick a time when the family is together. This may be at mealtime or in front of the television. The discussion doesn't have to take a lot of time, but you must have a consistent commitment to having it regularly.

Common Homework Time

Studies of successful students show that many families having more than one child have a communal homework time when all the children do their work at the kitchen table with the parent close by. This method allows older siblings to help younger children with particular problems. Some families make rules about when the children can leave the table so that the child who finishes last doesn't feel abandoned. As the children finish, they can draw or read while the others complete their work. Whether your children do their homework together or separately, there are advantages to having them all studying at the same time.

Learning Experiences

Learning experiences can include family activities or outings in which family members do something new or "educational" together. If the family is accustomed to going to the movies, try something new, such as a play. Try miniature golf or the challenge of indoor soccer. Frequent an art museum or a sushi bar. Talk about your experiences afterward. Even if no one enjoys the activity, it's still a meaningful learning experience.

Once you've decided what priorities, traditions, and experiences to have, sit down and discuss the "whys" and "hows" with your child. Alternatively, come up with a list of choices, and include your child in the selection process. At this get-together decide what the first learning experience, family common time, and/or homework procedures will be, and determine when they will occur, including date and time.

Challenges:

One of the biggest challenges of this priority-setting activity is that it may feel artificial and awkward to you at first. Parents rarely make plans for the family in such an intentional way. Your child may also experience this awkwardness. Since this is a learning experience for both of you, a willingness to work through the awkwardness is important. You may also have family routines that are fairly engrained, and these new ideas will run counter to them. It may take more than one attempt at the new routines or traditions to make them work and work well. Your first conversations may be lackluster or very short. That's perfectly all right — keep at it.

Opportunities:

Parents often note how little their children tell them or how little their children express themselves. There are often three reasons for this: lack of practice with self-expression, nothing interesting to talk about, and lack of opportunity or time. This prioritizing activity addresses each of these issues, providing ongoing experiences that can build family communication not just about learning and school, but in general. A parent who supports learning will improve the tenor of family communication and activities as well.

The Kaleidoscope Profile®

Conclusion

Now that you have finished this book, you understand that when children don't do well in school, the reason is often because their school or their parents don't recognize and/or address learning styles. With the assistance of The Kaleidoscope Profile®, you understand your child's learning style and how your own learning style differs or is the same.

Most importantly, you are equipped to be more involved in your child's learning and homework assignments.

You will be able to work with your child and her or his teacher to provide the support needed both at school and home. You understand why, when, and how much help to give your child with homework assignments and how to make the assignments more enjoyable for everyone involved.

You have found ways to improve your child's ability to do homework assignments, and as a result your child will be a confident and lifelong learner.

Now that you have read this book and you and your child have taken The Kaleidoscope Profile®, you may want to acquire *FIRE-UP* materials offered by Performance Learning Systems. With these materials you can encourage your child's skills to learn in the classroom and beyond. This resource, offered for parents, students, and teachers, is an excellent supplement to this study of learning styles.

Performance Learning Systems also offers a highly interactive online parenting course called "Homework and Study Strategies." This course is packed with practical strategies and exciting ideas that support the natural ways your child learns. The strategies are appropriate to use with children in first through sixth grades. The online course is also an excellent supplement to many activities in this book. Visit www.plsweb.com to register or learn more about this and other courses.

The reference materials at the end of this book can help you further support your child as a learner.

You have taken steps to provide your child with the skills of learning and an understanding of his or her own personal learning style. Continue to experiment, be patient, and have fun with your child in the years to come.

REFERENCES

Parental Involvement

Barbour, Chandler, & Nita, H. (1996). *Families, schools, and communities: Building partnerships for educating the children.* Upper Saddle River, NJ: Prentice Hall.

Barclay, Kathy, & Boone, Elizabeth. (1996). *The parent difference.* Arlington Heights, IL: Skylight Professional Development.

Batey, Carol S. (1996). *Parents are lifesavers: A handbook for parent involvement in school.* Thousand Oaks, CA: Corwin Press.

Benson, Peter L. (1998). *What kids need to succeed: Proven, practical ways to raise good kids.* Minneapolis, MN: Free Spirit.

Borba, Michele. (1994). *Home esteem builders: Activities designed to strengthen the partnership between the home and school.* Carson, CA: Jalmar Press.

Christopher, Cindy J. (1996). *Building parent-teacher communication.* Lanham, MD: Scarecrow Press.

Coloroso, Barbara. (Speaker). (1989). *Winning at parenting ... without beating your kids.* (Cassette Recording). New York: Avon Books.

Coloroso, Barbara. (1995). *Kids are worth it: Giving your child the gift of inner discipline.* New York: Avon Books.

Davidson, Alan, & Davidson, Robert. (1996). *How good parents raise great kids: The six essential habits of highly successful parents*. New York: Warner Books.

Decker, Larry E. (1994). *Getting parents involved in their children's education*. Arlington, VA: American Association of School Administrators.

Faber, Adele, & Mazlish, Elaine. (1999). *How to talk so kids will listen & listen so kids will talk*. New York: Rawson, Wade.

Hart, Louise, & Baumgardner, Kristen. (1993). *The winning family: Increasing self-esteem in your children and yourself*. Berkeley, CA: Celestial Arts.

Macfarlane, Eleanor. (1995). *Boost family involvement: How to make your program succeed under the new Title I guidelines*. Bloomington, IN: Grayson Bernard.

Price, Tom, & Price, Susan Crites. (1996). *The working parents' help book: Practical advice for dealing with the day-to-day challenges of kids and careers* (2nd ed.). Lawrenceville, NJ: Petersons Guides.

Stanmark, Jean Kerr, Thompson, Virginia, & Cossey, Ruth. (1996). *Family math*. Berkeley, CA: Lawrence Hall of Science.

Ziglar, Zig. (1996). *Raising positive kids in a negative world*. New York: Ballantine Books.

General Information on Learning

Adler, Mortimer J. (1984). *The Paideia Program: An educational syllabus* (1st ed.). Basingstoke Hampshire, England: Macmillan.

Ayers, A. Jean. (1979). *Sensory integration and the child*. Los Angeles: Western Psychological Services.

Bransford, John, Brown, Ann L., & Cocking, Rodney R. (Eds.). (2000). *How people learn: Brain, mind, experience, and school*. Washington, D.C: National Academy Press.

Butler, Kathleen A. (1988). *Learning and teaching style: In theory and practice* (2nd ed.). Columbia, CT: The Learner's Dimension.

Buzan, Tony. (1986). *Make the most of your mind.* New York: Simon & Schuster.

Goodman, Gretchen. (1995). *I can learn! Strategies and activities for gray-area children.* Peterborough, NH: Staff Development for Educators.

Gurian, Michael, Henly, Patricia, & Trueman, Terry. (2001). *Boys & girls learn differently: A guide for teachers and parents.* Somerset, NJ: Jossey-Bass.

Healy, Jane. (1994). *Your child's growing mind: A guide to learning and brain development from birth to adolescence.* New York: Doubleday.

Jensen, Eric. (1996). *Student success secrets kit* (4th ed.). Hauppauge, NY: Barron's Educational Series.

Jensen, Eric. (1997). *B's and A's in 30 days: Strategies for better grades in college.* Hauppauge, NY: Barron's Educational Series.

Kline, Peter. (1997). *The everyday genius: Restoring children's natural joy of learning, and yours too.* Arlington, VA: Great Ocean.

Kline, Peter, & Martel, Laurence D. (1994). *School success: The inside story.* Arlington, VA: Great Ocean.

The Learning Triangle. *The Heart of Teaching*, 77, 5.

Madden, Thomas L. (2001). *FIRE-UP your learning* (1st ed.). Las Vegas, NV: Stratigent Press.

Markova, Dawna, & Powell, Anne. (1992). *How your child is smart: A life-changing approach to learning.* Berkeley, CA: Conari Press.

Olsen, Janice Z. (1998). *Handwriting without tears* (7th ed.). Potomac, MD: Handwriting Without Tears.

Parnell, Dale P., & Leary, Margaret M. (1995). *Why do I have to learn this?* Waco, TX: CORD Communications.

Parry, Terrence, & Gregory, Gayle. (1998). *Designing brain-compatible learning.* Arlington Heights, IL: Skylight Professional Development.

Pelton, Ross. (1989). *Mind food & smart pills: A sourcebook for the vitamins, herbs, and drugs that can increase intelligence, improve memory, and prevent brain aging.* New York: Doubleday.

Silver, Harvey F., & Hanson, J. Robert. (1996). *Learning styles & strategies (The Unity in Diversity Series Vol. 1)* (2nd ed.). Trenton, NJ: Silver, Strong, & Associates, LLC.

Sylwester, Robert. (1995). *A celebration of neurons: An educator's guide to the human brain.* Alexandria, VA: Association for Supervision and Curriculum Development.

Tobias, Cynthia Ulrich. (1999). *Every child can succeed: Making the most of your child's learning style.* Colorado Springs, CO: Focus on the Family.

Walker, Morton. (1989). *The power of color.* East Rutherford, NJ: Avery Publishing Group.

Willis, Mariaemma, & Kindle-Hodson, Victoria. (1999). *Discover your child's learning style: Children learn in unique ways — Here's the key to every child's learning success.* Roseville, CA: Prima.

Learning Issues

Armstrong, Thomas. (1997). *The myth of the A.D.D. child: 50 ways to improve your child's behavior and attention span without drugs, labels, or coercion.* New York: Plume.

Cohen, Libby G. (Ed.). (1992). *Children with exceptional needs in regular classrooms.* Washington, D.C: National Education Association.

Davis, Ronald D., Braun, Eldon M., & Smith, Joan M. (1997). *The gift of dyslexia: Why some of the smartest people can't read and how they can learn*. New York: Berkley.

Dornbush, Marilyn P., & Pruitt, Sheryl K. (1995). *Teaching the tiger: A handbook for individuals in the education of students with attention deficit disorders, Tourette's syndrome or obsessive-compulsive disorder*. Duarte, CA: Hope Press.

Galbraithe, Judy, Espeland, Pamela, & Molnar, Albert. (1998). *The gifted kid's survival guide for ages 10 & under*. Minneapolis, MN: Free Spirit.

Harwell, Joan M. (2001). *Complete learning disabilities handbook: Ready to use strategies & activities for teaching students with learning disabilities* (2nd ed.). Minneapolis, MN: Center for Applied Research in Education.

Nelsen, Jane, Lott, Lynn, & Glenn, H. Stephen. (1999). *Positive discipline A-Z: Revised and expanded 2nd edition: From toddlers to teens, 1001 solutions to everyday parenting problems* (2nd ed.). Roseville, CA: Prima.

Rich, Dorothy. (1998). *MegaSkills: Building children's achievement for the information age*. Boston: Houghton Mifflin.

Rief, Sandra F. (1993). *How to reach and teach ADD/ADHD children: Practical techniques, strategies, and interventions for helping children with attention problems and hyperactivity*. Minneapolis, MN: Center for Applied Research in Education.

Winebrenner, Susan, & Espeland, Pamela. (1996). *Teaching kids with learning difficulties in the regular classroom: Strategies every teacher can use to challenge and motivate struggling students*. Minneapolis, MN: Free Spirit.

Discover Your Children's Learning Styles!
Using The Kaleidoscope Profile®

Student profiles (grades 3-12)
Adult profiles (Workplace and Educator)
Directions and Applications booklet

The Student version of **The Kaleidoscope Profile®** is a useful tool that will give you information about how your children learn and what they value. The Workplace version will tell how you learn and work best so you can compare your styles with those of your children.

The profile uses colorful stickers to indicate 12 different learning and working styles. The sticker approach to profiling is a vast improvement over paper-and-pencil profiles. Everyone finds this profile fun to take and easy to score.

When you know how your children learn best, you can help them:
- improve the way they study.
- learn better.
- prepare for tests.
- figure out how to listen in class and take notes.
- relate better to teachers, siblings, and friends.
- convey their learning styles to teachers and tutors.
- And more!

As one parent said: "Understanding my son's learning styles — and my own — gave me useful tools for working with him at home. Now he can use learning techniques that match his style."

Order directly from Performance Learning Systems through the PLS Bookstore. Four versions of the profile are available:
- Student (grades 3-6) • Student (grades 7-12)
- Workplace (adult and college students)
- Educator (for classroom teachers)
  - 800-506-9996
  - Fax: 530-265-8629
  - Full-Order Web Site: www.plsbookstore.com
  - E-mail: info@plsbookstore.com